EVERYONE DOES BETTER WITH A COACH
Practical Solutions For Kidmin & NextGen Leaders

Jim Wideman with
Yancy Wideman Richmond, Corey Jones, Brittany Nelson,
Corinne Noble, Vicki Abbott, Tom Bump, Andrea Goslee,
Jeffrey Hunter, Tyler Thompson, Rachel Pilcher,
Emily Saum, & Stacey Brooks

A Jim Wideman Ministries, Inc. Publication
jimwideman.com
Jim Wideman Ministries, Inc
2441Q Old Fort Pkwy #354
Murfreesboro, TN 37128
Helping leaders think differently
at home, at church, and in everyday life!

Everyone Does Better With a Coach: Practical Solutions For Kidmin & NextGen Leaders

Copyright © by Jim Wideman.

All Rights Reserved.

No portion of this book may be reproduced in any form without written permission from the publisher or author, except as permitted by U.S. copyright law.

Published by Jim Wideman Ministries, Inc.
2441Q Old Fort Pkwy #354
Murfreesboro, TN 37128

Printed in the United States of America

Cover Design and Book Layout by Nicole Jones, kneecoalgrace@gmail.com

Edited by Tina Houser

Scripture quotations marked (NIV) are taken from the Holy Bible, New International Version®, NIV®. Copyright © 1973, 1978, 1984, 2011 by Biblica, Inc.™ Used by permission of Zondervan. All rights reserved worldwide. www.zondervan.comThe "NIV" and "New International Version" are trademarks registered in the United States Patent and Trademark Office by Biblica, Inc.™

Scripture quotations marked NLT are taken from the Holy Bible, New Living Translation, Copyright © 1996, 2004, 2015 by Tyndale House Foundation. Used by permission of Tyndale House Publishers, Inc., Carol Stream, Illinois 60188. All rights reserved.

Scripture quotations marked NKJV taken from the New King James Version®. Copyright © 1982 by Thomas Nelson. Used by permission. All rights reserved.

Scripture quotations are from The ESV® Bible (The Holy Bible, English Standard Version®), © 2001 by Crossway, a publishing ministry of Good News Publishers. Used by permission. All rights reserved.

ISBN 978-0-9838306-9-6
ISBN (eBook) 978-0-9855322-0-8

Visit our website at jimwideman.com

Table of Contents

Introducton 7

1 Stepping Into A New Role 17

2 Organizing Your Time, Tasks, and Leadership 29

3 Elevate Your Leadership 39

4 Healing Church Hurt 49

5 Serving Your Leader 59

6 Hearing God's Voice 69

7 Empowering Volunteers 79

8 Asking Better Questions 89

9 Managing Leadership Transitions 99

10 Helping Your Own Kids Love Jesus and His Church 109

11 Caring for Your Heart 119

12 There's No Junior Holy Spirit 129

13 Small Church, Big Impact 141

14 Leading as a Young Leader 153

15 Making Your Service Dazzle 163

16 Making Worship Better 175

17 Bridging the Gap Between
Kids and Students 185

18 Say "No" to Silos 195

19 Hey Staff,
Can We All Get Along? 203

20 Applying What You've Learned 213

Meet Jim Wideman 221

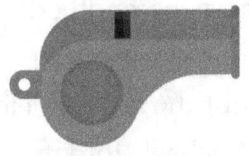

Introducing 5-3-1
Jim Wideman

Thanks for reading *Everyone Does Better with a Coach!* I truly believe this statement with all my heart. It's not just a catchy tagline or a slogan. It's been one of the secrets of my own personal success as both a minister and a parent. I'm a product of the combined influences of the many coaches in my life. Over my leadership journey, I've never seen a situation where this statement wasn't 100% true: "Everyone Does Better with a Coach!" I am thankful for all the coaches and mentors I've had throughout my life—from Little League to each of the seven pastors I've served. Each one has deposited something into me that made me better. I love Proverbs 27:17 (NIV): "As iron sharpens iron, so one person sharpens another!" This describes the true value of coaching.

Think about the best athletes of all time—the GOATs—Michael Jordan, LeBron James, Simone Biles, Tom Brady, Caitlin Clark and Pete Sampras, to name a few. No matter how great they are, they all have one thing in common: they all had a coach ... and not just one coach. Some also had specialty coaches working on specific elements of their game to achieve better performance and results.

It's not just in sports. It's true in business. It's true in music. (My daughter Yancy's vocal coach here in Nashville is also Beyoncé's vocal coach.) It's true in the health and fitness industry. I've benefited so much from trainers and my medical team over the last few years. And it's also true in ministry. Especially in ministry today, coaches are coming alongside different leaders in all types of ministries, helping them see their dreams come true. Did you know there are over

11,500 career coaches currently employed in the United States alone?

When I started in ministry to children and youth 50 years ago, there wasn't much available in the world of specialty training. Most of us in the early days did whatever we could think up to minister to kids and teens. We did what those who had taught us as kids and teens did. When you heard about what someone across the country was doing, you called and picked their brain, or you visited them to see for yourself firsthand. Then, out of the blue, conferences and seminars showed up annually, and most of them you had to travel great distances to attend. I have to be honest: I'm thankful for the conferences I attended. They molded and helped shape my ministry, but over the last 25 years that I have been coaching both groups and individuals, the results have been much more effective and have caused me to see faster results with lasting benefits than just through conferences alone.

Thanks to technology and the wonderful

world of the internet, training as well as group and personal coaching, are easier to take advantage of and more affordable than ever. Imagine having a personal cheerleader, a guide, a teacher, and a mentor all rolled into one—that's what a great coach brings to your life. Whether you're hitting the gym, climbing the corporate ladder, or even navigating the complexities of ministry, a coach can help you go farther and faster than you ever thought possible. That's why we created this book. I believe that you can maximize your potential in any area faster with coaching than you can achieve on your own.

In January of 2024, after years of offering coaching for those in Kidmin and NextGen ministry, I offered my first Coaching for Coaches Group. The Lord assembled some of the sharpest and brightest leaders from all over the country who I have ever had the privilege of working with. Each one has a burning desire to help others achieve more through coaching. Along with other future Coaching for Coaches groups, I formed a coaching network to pass on my coaching legacy. It consists of the creation of resources like this book and also group and individual coaching with the best coaches from my coaching tree.

Within this book, we identified some of the biggest problems found in Kidmin and NextGen Ministry today. Each coach will give you five practical solutions you can adapt now to help you do ministry better. Each coach will give you three questions to ask yourself that will help you implement these five solutions. Then, we'll help you get started by asking you to identify your first step. Psalm 37:23-24 (NIV) says, "The steps of a righteous man are ordered by the Lord." If Jesus leads us in steps, it's important for us to think in steps, and all you need to get started is to know the first step. That's what 5-3-1 means.

If any of us can help you formulate a complete plan, feel free to contact us for more coaching. Our contact info is listed at the end of each chapter.

That all sounds great, Jim, but I've got one big question: What makes a great coach anyway? What makes y'all special? That's a great question. Let me give you five reasons you should listen to the solutions we have provided here.

1. We are lifelong learners

Good coaches are perpetual students of life. They don't just share old war stories. They bring fresh insights and challenges to keep you on your toes.

2. We are guides, not counselors

While counselors help you unpack the past, coaches are all about future success. They're your navigators, charting the course for where you're headed next.

3. We are process devotees

Forget quick fixes! Great coaches are in it for the long haul, helping you rethink and revamp your processes for lasting change.

4. We are performance enhancers

Unlike consultants who swoop in to solve a problem, coaches stick around, focusing on boosting your overall performance over time.

5. We are beyond mentors

Sure, mentors offer advice, and we'll be dishing out a lot of it, but coaches go further—they're hands-on, proactive, and always in your corner, pushing you to excel.

Each of us wants to share our secret sauce to help you be more effective!

In *Everyone Does Better with a Coach!*, you'll learn how to set an example in leadership, service, and continuous learning. Get ready for a fun, engaging read, filled with practical tips and heartwarming anecdotes that will make you laugh, think, and most importantly, grow.

So buckle up! This book is your ticket to unlocking your full potential with the help of some great coaches and, even better, friends. Ready to get started? Let's dive in and discover how everyone, yes everyone, does better with a coach!

3 Suggestions for You

1. Take your time and read each chapter. View that chapter as a coaching session with that coach on that particular subject.

2. Before going straight to the next chapter, take the time to answer the three questions. The more you think through your answers, the more you'll get out of the chapter.

3. Ask Jesus to show you the first step. I've found most people want a pill but what they need is a process. Every good process starts with the first step. You may want Z, but the road to Z starts with A.

First Step

If you're ready to do the work, turn the page and let the coaching begin! Thanks again for joining us on this journey.

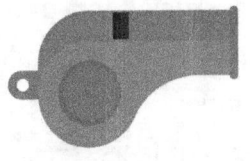

1
Stepping Into A New Role
Jim Wideman

It's your first day in a new role at a different church. The welcome party is over, and now you're sitting alone in your office, wondering what to do next. The steps you take in the next few months will shape your ministry for years to come. Here's how to start strong, whether you're building a ministry from scratch or stepping into a role that is well established.

1. Observe and Learn

Do nothing drastic at first: Your first impulse might be to start implementing changes immediately, but resist this urge. Spend the initial months observing and asking questions.

This period is crucial for understanding the church's culture, the existing children's ministry, and the expectations of the senior pastor, parents, kids, and volunteers.

Understanding the landscape: Find out what has been done before and how people define a "great" ministry. It's likely that these definitions will vary significantly among different groups. By observing carefully, you'll be able to piece together a comprehensive view of what's valued and what needs improvement. Ask questions like:

- What are the strengths of the current program?
- What have been the biggest challenges?
- How do different stakeholders (pastor, parents, volunteers) view the ministry?

Building connections: Develop relationships with the leadership team and other staff members. These connections are vital for your success. Schedule lunches or coffee meetings to learn their perspectives and goals. Show genuine interest in their work and share your vision for the ministry that you oversee. This will help you align your efforts with the church's overall mission and build trust.

2. Make Small Improvements

Start with small, visible changes: Once you've spent some time understanding the landscape, identify a small but impactful change that you can make. This could be something as simple as reorganizing a storage area, updating your graphics, or improving a check-in process. The key is to choose something that will have a noticeable positive impact without requiring significant resources or time.

Building trust through action: Fixing a minor issue demonstrates your commitment to improving the ministry and shows that you're attentive to the needs of the community. It builds trust and establishes your credibility. People will start to see you as someone who is capable and worth listening to, which is crucial as you plan for larger changes.

Joining and supporting the team: Take time to understand and respect the work of other ministry leaders. Recognize that you are part of a larger team, and your success is interconnected with theirs. If the youth group leaves the shared space in chaos, for example, approach the youth pastor with respect and a collaborative spirit. Offer to help find a solution that works for both of you. This mutual respect fosters a cohesive ministry team.

3. Set Clear Goals and Plans

Define your vision: Work closely with the senior pastor to understand their vision for the ministries that you oversee. Identify the resources available to you, including leadership, tools, curriculum, furniture, and space. Once you have a clear understanding, write down your current assessment and future goals for the ministry. This written plan should summarize where you are now and where you want to go. Every good vision includes both.

Sharing and refining your plan: Present your written plan to the leadership above you for feedback. This step ensures that your goals align with the church's overall vision and gives the leadership an opportunity to fine-tune your direction. Clear, documented goals provide a roadmap for your ministry and help you communicate your vision to volunteers and parents.

Communicate effectively: Effective communication is essential. Create regular updates and newsletters for parents and volunteers. Share what you're teaching, upcoming events, and any changes to the schedule. Use multiple channels (email, web pages, social media) to ensure that your messages reach everyone. Regular communication builds trust and keeps everyone informed and engaged.

4. Build and Empower Your Team

Develop job descriptions and roles: Clear job descriptions are essential for every volunteer. Every volunteer wants to know "What do you want me to do, and how do you want me to do it?" Start by writing your own job description and submitting it to the senior leadership for approval. Once you have clarity on your role, create job descriptions for each volunteer position. Share these descriptions with your team so everyone understands their responsibilities and how they fit into the bigger picture.

Encourage leadership and involvement: Mentor and coach your volunteers to take on leadership roles. See yourself as a coach and a mentor, regardless of the size of your team. Encourage volunteers to step up and take ownership of their roles. Delegation is important, but strive for duplication—instilling your heart and passion in others so they can replicate your leadership style and vision.

Building a supportive culture: Foster a culture of mutual respect and support. Encourage volunteers to respect each other and work together towards common goals. Celebrate successes and provide constructive feedback to help your team grow. A supportive culture attracts and retains dedicated volunteers, which is essential for the success of your ministry.

5. Lead well!

Manage resources wisely: Learn the budgeting process and plan your financial needs early. Find out how budgets are done, who is responsible, when they are created, and what the approval process involves. This knowledge will help you create a realistic budget that supports your ministry goals. When creating your budget, start by defining what you want to accomplish with your children's ministry. Then, develop a plan that meets those goals and estimate the costs involved.

Be visible and engaged: Participate actively in worship services. Your presence sets an example for your volunteers and shows that you are committed to the spiritual life of the church. Sit down front, be visible, and engage in worship enthusiastically. This visibility reinforces the importance of worship and spiritual growth for your volunteers.

Use the church calendar: Coordinate with other ministries by using the church's master calendar. This helps avoid scheduling conflicts and increases participation in children's ministry events. Families won't have to choose between conflicting meetings, making it easier for them to be involved.

Stay adaptable and open: Be creative and open to new ideas that fit the unique needs of your new church. Avoid the temptation to replicate past programs without first assessing their relevance. Always start by identifying the needs of your children and volunteers, and then find or create programs that address those needs.

Your first year in any new ministry position is crucial for establishing a strong foundation for your ministry. Focus on building relationships, making small but meaningful improvements, and aligning your efforts with the church's mission. Remember, ministry is a marathon, not a sprint. Take your time, stay connected with your family, and lead both at home and at church with dedication and grace.

By observing and learning, making small improvements, setting clear goals, building and empowering your team, and planning for practicalities and growth, you can ensure a successful and impactful first year. These steps will help you build a thriving children's ministry that nurtures faith, fosters community, and supports the spiritual growth of your church's youngest members.

3 Questions to Ask Yourself

1. Why should you spend the first few months just observing and asking questions instead of diving into changes right away?

2. How can setting clear goals and keeping good communication with your team and church leaders help make your children's ministry awesome?

3. What are some fun and effective ways to build up your volunteer team and encourage them to take on leadership roles?

First Step

What will be your first step to observe and learn in your new role?

_____

_____

About Jim

Jim Wideman has been helping ministry leaders thrive for a half century. He's currently The Executive Pastor of Ministries at Conduit Church in Franklin, Tennessee. He also offers group and individual coaching throughout the year and has authored over 15 books for NextGen ministry. Find out more about his resources and coaching at:

jimwideman.com

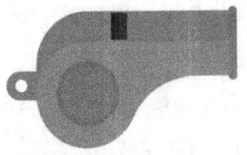

2
Organizing Your Time, Tasks, and Leadership
Brittany Nelson

When I say "organized," what comes to mind? A supply closet with clearly labeled bins stacked neatly in alphabetical order? A color-coded calendar that tells you exactly what to do and when? A clean desk with not even a paperclip out of place? Each leader's level of organization will vary, but being organized is a fundamental element of solid leadership and a thriving ministry.

Whether administration is one of your spiritual gifts or your biggest challenge, organization is vital for growth, and it goes beyond your supply closet to encompass your time and tasks. We see biblical examples of organization and planning in creation, Noah and the ark, the tribes of Israel, Moses, Joshua, Acts and the early church, Paul, Jesus' ministry, and even in the character of God Himself. So obviously, organization and planning are important to God. He is a God of order, and as a leader, He calls you to mirror this pursuit of structure.

Organization in leadership and ministry allows you to be a good steward of the gifts, time, and resources God has given you. So how can you get more organized?

1. Evaluate and prioritize

Start by taking a look at where you currently stand with organization. Are there any areas or spaces in particular that need some extra attention? Are your supplies easily accessible for you and your team? Is your office cleaned up after that last big event, or are there still boxes of extra supplies piled on the floor? Think beyond just your physical spaces to your time and task list too.

One of my favorite things to do when I feel unorganized or overwhelmed is to complete a brain dump. A brain dump is dumping the contents of your mind onto paper to clear out the mental clutter and give you the clarity to move forward. (On DeeperKidMin.com, search "Brain dump" to find a 4-step brain dump exercise that can be applied to a specific event or project, your overall ministry, or life in general, to help you reduce stress and maximize productivity.) Once you write all your to-do's on paper, you can organize and prioritize them. Looking at your task list, what can you delegate, what can you schedule for the future, and what can you eliminate? Keep your goals and ministry mission statement nearby to help you identify what tasks deserve your time and attention.

2. Look at your physical spaces

Next, take a look at your physical spaces, particularly those you share with others. Take time twice a year to do some deep cleaning in your supply closet. Take inventory of what you have, what supplies you may need to purchase, and what items you can donate or trash. Look at your large and small group spaces. Are they clutter-free to reduce distraction and foster engagement with kids and volunteers? Does your check-in area create an open traffic flow, and do visitors know exactly where to go?

Then, look at your desk and office. Confession: my desk is typically a cluttered scene of organized chaos. I have to be very intentional about clearing off my desk and putting things in the proper place rather than letting them pile up over time. But remember that your office reflects you and your leadership; you'll appear more professional and trustworthy if your space is organized and neat.

3. Cultivate a team and delegate

I've always said trying to do ministry alone is like trying to ride a seesaw by yourself. It might work for a while, but eventually, you burn out, and it's not much fun. Part of being more organized is cultivating a team to help you make ministry happen. Create an organizational structure for your ministry by listing all the roles needed to make your ministry happen. Don't limit yourself to the positions you think you can fill—dream big! Once you have your list, organize them into teams and identify leadership roles. You may have teams like a kids' greeter team, nursery team, preschool team, elementary team, teaching team, supply team, etc., and then leadership roles for each of those teams. Creating job descriptions for each role allows you to more easily invite people to the team and ensures that everyone is on the same page when it comes to expectations.

4. Leverage digital tools

I wrote an entire book about leveraging the digital world for discipleship in children's ministries called *Time to Update: 7 Areas to Integrate Digital Discipleship into Your Children's Ministry Strategy*. I will share a few tips here. Use digital tools to help you stay organized with your files and time. A digital calendar is a must, and I love using my digital to-do list that syncs across all my devices. File-sharing tools allow you to easily share and store pictures, lesson plans, media, and more with your staff and team. Use digital tools to help you keep track of attendance and streamline communication with the team you created in the last step and the families you serve. The digital world offers you ways to be more organized than ever before. Wise leaders take advantage of the tools available to them.

5. Develop routines and habits

Organizing is like laundry: even after a big load, there will always be more to do. After you complete the initial wave of organizing, identify small habits and routines you can implement to help you stay organized. Regularly block off time to evaluate and prioritize your tasks. Spend 15 minutes each day celebrating what you accomplished and preparing for what you need to accomplish tomorrow. That way, you don't spend a lot of time upfront just figuring out what you need to do. You can jump right in, and it helps your brain focus on what needs to get done instead of where to start. Make a habit of cleaning up after big events (and even Sunday mornings) within 24 hours of the event. Regularly take time off and organize your calendar in a way that gives you extra rest after a particularly busy season. The more organized you are, the easier it is to take time off.

Ultimately, organization leads to longevity in ministry—for yourself, for your volunteers, and even for your church after you've moved on. When you intentionally improve the organization of your time, tasks, and supplies, you set yourself and your ministry up for healthy growth.

3 Questions to Ask Yourself

1. When can you make time on your calendar to evaluate and prioritize? Block off time now and make an appointment with yourself to do just that. Looking at your current list of tasks and responsibilities, what can you schedule for the future, delegate, or eliminate?

2. What digital tool(s) might help you become more organized? Ask other staff members or ministry leaders what digital tools they use, and

check out deeperkidmin.com/timetoupdatebook for a deep dive into using digital tools to increase effectiveness in ministry.

3. What habit(s) can you form to help you streamline your organization processes?

First Step

What's your first step to getting more organized in your leadership and ministry?

_____

_____

About Brittany

Brittany Nelson is an author, speaker, and the creator of DeeperKidMin.com, an online hub of downloadable resources made FOR children's ministry leaders BY children's ministry leaders. She loves leading the 2nd/3rd grade small group at her church and volunteering with her husband's youth group. Her other adventures include being a mom to the two sweetest girls, reading as many books as she can, and drinking lots of herbal tea. One day, she hopes to run the Disney Half Marathon dressed as her favorite princess, Belle. Connect with Brittany on social media at @deeperkidmin and find her online at:

deeperkidmin.com

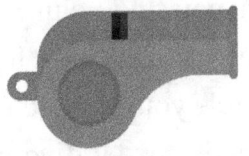

3
Elevate Your Leadership
Jim Wideman

Leadership isn't just about having a title; it's about inspiring and guiding others in a way that's meaningful and impactful. The Bible gives us some great advice on being a leader in 1 Peter 5:2-4 (NIV) which says, "Be shepherds of God's flock that is under your care, serving as overseers—not because you must, but because you are willing, as God wants you to be; not greedy for money, but eager to serve; not lording it over those entrusted to you, but being examples to the flock." Leaders are examples! I hear you out there saying I thought leadership is influence. It's more than that. You must identify what you want those you serve to know and be when they grow up. Then, you find volunteers to be examples of those things to the kids. It starts with you being the example yourself to those you lead.

In this chapter we'll dive into five practical things you can do now to up your leadership game and become the leader you're meant to be.

1. Be someone worth following

First things first … If you want people to follow you, be someone worth following. Live out your faith! True leadership starts with personal integrity and Jesus modeled this perfectly. Here's how you can follow His example. Know the Word and do it! It's not enough to just read the Bible; live it out in your daily life. James 1:22 (NIV) is plain—Be doers of the Word and not hearers only. Love deeply! Show genuine love for God, your family, your team, and your community. People are drawn to authentic love.

Flow with authority. You can tell a lot about a leader by how they respect and work well with those in authority over them. If you're going to be someone worth following, you must constantly keep check on your spiritual health. Your personal relationship with Jesus is the cornerstone of your leadership. Two questions I ask myself and those I lead, as well as those I coach, on a regular basis: "Has there ever been a time when you were more in love with Jesus than you are right now?" And "How's your prayer life?" A strong prayer life fuels your spiritual and leadership journey.

2. Set the example you want others to follow

Leadership is about actions, not just words. Your team will mirror your behavior, so make sure you're setting the right example. Start by working hard as well as working smart. Something I've modeled and told my children and grands their whole life is, "There might be people with more talent, but no one should outwork you!" A strong work ethic is contagious. Effective leaders teach, model, and evaluate. Show your team how to succeed by doing it yourself and then help them do the same. Teach always: Share your knowledge and skills with your team. Be sure to model by demonstrating the behaviors and attitudes you want to see. Regularly assess the progress others are making and always be willing to provide constructive feedback along the way.

I tell my staff I've got some good news and bad news for you. The good news is I will never ask you to do something I'm not willing to do. That's some pretty good news, so what's the bad news? The bad news is there's just about nothing that I am not willing to do. If you work with me, you're going to get after it, but I'll be right there with you setting the example.

3. Learn how to work smart

Being efficient and productive is key to effective leadership. Here's how to make the most of your time: Use the right tools. Invest in tools that help you stay organized and efficient.

Whether it's a great planner or productivity apps, find what works for you.

Break down large tasks into manageable to-dos and prioritize them. Planning ahead helps you stay on top of things. Planning must always go before action. Remember, it wasn't raining when Noah started working on the ark. Identify time-wasters and delegate tasks when possible. Trust your team with responsibilities to maximize efficiency and develop their skills. Regularly review your tasks to eliminate time-wasters.

Trust your team to handle tasks and free up your time for more important matters. That's the power of delegation. For more ways to become a master of time management, check out my book, *Beat The Clock*, at jimwideman.com.

4. Communicate like a pro

Good communication is crucial for successful leadership. Here's how to improve your communication skills.

Learn to respond promptly. After everything is said and done, there's usually more said than done. Do more, talk less.

Return calls quickly. Make sure calls are returned promptly, either by you or someone else. You can instantly raise your leadership level by answering your phone. Especially youth pastors!

Manage emails efficiently. Set specific times to check and respond to emails. When possible, aim to do it within 24 hours. Always follow up on conversations with an email to ensure clarity and accountability. Utilize various communication channels like websites, texting, brochures, and e-newsletters to reach your audience. Never put all your eggs in one basket.

Be accessible. Make yourself available and approachable. This builds trust and openness. When possible, stay out of the green room and head to the lobby where the people are. You'll see the difference it makes instantly.

5. Show up and be prepared

Punctuality and preparedness are signs of a committed and effective leader. Here's how to ensure you're always ready.

Arrive early. Show up at least 30 minutes before everyone else. This gives you time to set up and be prepared to greet your team as they arrive.

Set the scene. Make sure your facilities reflect your vision and are ready to inspire those who arrive. This includes the restrooms. You have the facilities looking good, now it's time to make sure you look presentable.

Your appearance matters. Dress appropriately and ensure that you represent your pastor and leadership well. Dress to impress. A great rule to live by is when in doubt, it's better to be slightly overdressed than underdressed.

Raising your leadership level doesn't have to be complicated. By being someone worth following, setting a strong example, maximizing your productivity, communicating effectively, and always being prepared, you can elevate your leadership and make a lasting impact. By implementing these steps and continuously seeking ways to improve, you will become a more effective and inspiring leader. Leadership is a journey, not a destination. Keep growing, learning, and leading with excellence.

3 Questions to Ask Yourself

1. Of the 5 things listed above, which one of them are you currently doing the best?

2. Looking again at the list, which one needs the most work?

3. Thinking about your prayer life and your overall spiritual care, what grade would you give yourself right now?

First Step

What's your first step in making the needed improvements you've identified from these three questions?

_____

_____

About Jim

Jim Wideman has been helping ministry leaders thrive for a half century. He's currently The Executive Pastor of Ministries at Conduit Church in Franklin, Tennessee. He also offers group and individual coaching throughout the year and has authored over 15 books for NextGen ministry. Find out more about his resources and coaching at:

jimwideman.com

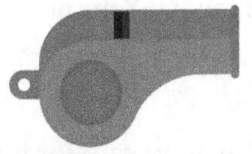

4
Healing Church Hurt
Tom Bump

As a ministry leader, you learn sooner or later that sometimes sheep bite… and sometimes other shepherds can throw stones… and being in leadership can hurt.

As someone who has been in ministry for a while and has seen the good, bad, and the ugly, I want to share five things you can do to heal from those hurts.

1. You must name the specific hurt and treat it properly

A common mistake is not addressing the hurt right away. Instead, you either try to bury it down inside or you go the opposite way and air it out on social media. Your heart needs spiritual first aid to heal, so that you can lead renewed and restored.

The right way to care for it is to talk about the hurt, and if possible, talk directly with the person who hurt you. Read Matthew 18 for guidance on how to approach this conversation. Many times, you discover healing in those hard conversations and you gain the benefits of reconciliation. Sometimes, you must take time away first; then, when ready, have that talk.

During this time, allow yourself to feel the emotions that come with the hurt, such as sadness, anger, or confusion. It's important to grieve any loss of trust or community. Find healthy ways to process these emotions, like journaling or talking to a counselor or a trusted friend. Sometimes, a trained counselor can help guide you through the process of sorting out the hurt and offering a path towards healing.

2. You must practice biblical forgiveness

Forgive those who have hurt you and also forgive yourself. Forgiveness helps you let go of resentment and move forward positively.

I've found that when I practice forgiveness, I find new freedom from the hurt. It moves me beyond dwelling on the past and looking forward to the future. While I know forgiveness doesn't come easy, it is required and Jesus commanded us to it in Matthew 6:14-15 NIV. You are to forgive as you have been forgiven. Sometimes, it may require you to separate or create boundaries. When you forgive, you release what was done to you and find freedom from that hurt.

I encourage you, if you are hurting right now, to ask God how you can forgive and release those wounds so that He may bring healing to your soul. Never forget God is always good, even when His people are bad. He's for you and you are not finished yet.

3. You need to change your mind

The third step towards healing from hurt is setting your mind to think about new things. When I was hurting at my lowest point, I couldn't stop thinking about what was hurting and who did the hurting. My heart was angry and bitterness was starting to set in. It had all kinds of negative effects on my mind and physically on my body. I needed to start changing my mind if I wanted to change the direction I was going.

Romans 12 challenges you to renew your mind daily. That is where I started to move beyond the hurt that was holding me hostage. I began to create new thoughts, a new playlist of sorts, that when I began to wrestle with thinking of the past, I replaced it with something new—something healthier and holier than my present thoughts. Philippians 2 tells you to have the mind of Christ, and later in chapter 4 you are given a whole list of new things. "Finally brothers, whatever is true, whatever is noble, whatever is right, whatever is pure, whatever is lovely, whatever is admirable, if anything is excellent or praiseworthy, think about such things."

When you fill yourself with Jesus and His mindset, you have no room for the negative. You have no room to be angry or bitter or hold a grudge which never allows for the hurt to heal. So, which playlist do you want in your head?

This is not an easy process, but healing takes time and it takes heart work. It takes you being intentional and having some support along the way. You don't have to walk this valley alone. Give this hurt to God and commit it to Him. Stop trying to solve it with your own understanding.

4. Don't walk through the valley of hurt alone

Get someone to walk through the valley season with you. When I was hurting, I searched to find a safe place to talk, vent, and get wise counsel. It was hard, but I found a counselor who understood what it was like to be in ministry leadership. He helped guide me through some hard things. He helped me see a path that if I stayed on it and trusted the process, it would bring me to a place of help.

It inspired me to start a ministry for leaders who needed that safe place. I call it restoring-leaders.org and it's a mission to help those who are hurting and burned out from ministry find themselves again. If I can help you find your way through the valley, please reach out.

5. Develop spiritual habits for renewal and restoration

I've found that healing from hurt took developing new spiritual habits or disciplines. The most powerful and restorative for me were silence, stillness, and rest.

Silence is not just about stopping your speech. It's about being in a place to listen… to allow the Holy Spirit to speak in His still small voice… to allow the Spirit to show you His grace, mercy, and love. Silence is about hearing from God how much you are valued and known by Him and how He wants to bring you healing.

Stillness is a heart attitude. Like silence, it is receptive to hearing from God. It's putting yourself in a place to release, restore, and renew yourself, your calling, and your mission. When you practice stillness, you are submitting to God for His direction, and you're willing to follow what He shows you to do in obedience.

Rest is allowing your physical body to stop. I don't understand how leaders today think being worn out is a badge of honor or something to brag about. You need to stop being so arrogant to think you can cheat your days off and not rest. I say this as nicely as I can. If Jesus the Son of God stopped and rested, and if God the Father stopped all He was doing to rest, you my friend MUST learn to set aside everything and rest.

One reason many struggle with hurt, depression, discouragement, and the desire to quit ministry is a lack of obedience when it comes to these three things.

3 Questions to Ask Yourself

1. Have I acknowledged and addressed the specific hurt(s) I've experienced, and have I talked directly to the person who hurt me?

2. Am I actively practicing biblical forgiveness towards those who have hurt me and toward myself, to release any resentment or hurt and move forward in a healthy way?

3. Have I intentionally practiced renewing my mind by focusing on the positive, uplifting thoughts and developing spiritual habits such as silence, stillness, and rest for renewal and restoration?

First Step

What will be the first step you take to deal with any church hurt you've encountered?

_____

_____

About Tom

Tom Bump has been in ministry for over 35 years and currently serves ministry leaders through coaching and his membership community kidminplus.net. His passion work is to help hurting and burned out leaders find their way through hard seasons. He founded Restoring Leaders and has written *Valleys Over Mountains: a guide through the hard seasons*. Find out more at:

restoringleaders.org

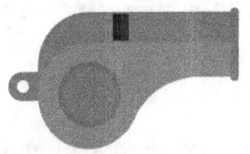

5
Serving Your Leader
Corey Jones

If you're like most people, you stepped into your role to do a job and there's a leader above you on the org chart. This leader isn't perfect (hint: neither are you), but God has placed them in this position for such a time as this. You can approach your leader with a prideful attitude, or you can heed the words of Jesus: "The greatest among you must be a servant" Matthew 23:11 (NLT).

The way you serve your leader reflects your service to God. As we explore five ways to better serve your leader, remember to "Work willingly at whatever you do, as though you were working for the Lord rather than for people" Colossians 3:23 (NLT).

1. Be willing to change

So, how willing to change are you? You can probably find an assessment online with 10 simple questions, but I encourage you to check your heart posture and ask the Holy Spirit for counsel.

You can serve your leader best when your heart is open and willing to pivot in whatever direction the Holy Spirit is leading. Perhaps God is calling you to change from a complainer to a problem solver? Maybe you need to change by anticipating the needs of others instead of focusing on your own desires? Or, perhaps God is asking you to become more flexible with your own plans and to instead trust the Holy Spirit?

"Since we are living by the Spirit, let us follow the Spirit's leading in every part of our lives. Let us not become conceited, or provoke one another, or be jealous of one

another" Galatians 5:25-26 (NLT).

2. Understand your leader

Do you find yourself on a different page than your leader? Are you speaking different languages? Part of serving your leader well involves learning their personality and figuring out how to communicate in a way they can understand.

When I wanted to pitch the idea of launching a preteen ministry at my church, I knew understanding my pastor was going to be important. Instead of walking in unscheduled, I picked a time that fit in his schedule. Instead of speaking my natural language of statistics and square feet, I spoke my pastor's language and shared personal stories of kids who would hear the Good News. I explained how current preteens feel in our environment and cast a vision of what could be in the future. Understanding my pastor gave me a solid foundation to start the conversation.

Serve your leader by understanding their vision and goals and aligning your efforts with the ministry's direction. Be a joyful collaborator and seek to build unity in the whole church. Because you seek to understand your leader, when you walk into their office with smart timing and clear communication, the interaction will bring glory and honor to God and further both your ministry efforts.

> *"Obey your spiritual leaders, and do what they say. Their work is to watch over your souls, and they are accountable to God. Give them reason to do this with joy and not with sorrow. That would certainly not be for your benefit" Hebrews 13:17 (NLT).*

3. Have integrity

How would you describe yourself—trustworthy, consistent? Do you follow through on your commitments and deliver on your promises? Consider how your leader perceives you:

someone reliable or as someone with excuses. Serving your leader and your church best requires integrity. Sometimes, the most impactful service isn't grand gestures but simply doing what you said you would do. Integrity also means owning your mistakes. Sometimes, the most impactful service is humble acts like confessing sins or repenting.

> *"If you are faithful in little things, you will be faithful in large ones. But if you are dishonest in little things, you won't be honest with greater responsibilities"* Luke 16:10 (NLT).

4. Enthusiastic contribution

Have you ever been driving a rental car when the service engine light came on and you simply ignored it? There is a stark difference between renting and owning. Similarly, you serve your leader well by enthusiastically contributing to the ministry as an owner, and not just your area, but the ministry as a whole. Don't allow laziness and silos to creep in. Instead, be like David and draw strength from the Lord to give your best with a grateful heart.

> *"Brothers and sisters, we urge you to warn those who are lazy. Encourage those who are timid. Take tender care of those who are weak. Be patient with everyone"*
> *1 Thessalonians 5:14 (NLT).*

5. Extend grace and encouragement

Have you noticed the leaders you enjoy being around are often the most encouraging? That's certainly true for me. Leaders full of grace and encouragement resemble Jesus, making them the best kind of leaders. One key way you can serve your leader is by recognizing their efforts and using your platform to celebrate ministry successes. Let them know you appreciate their leadership and share wins with them from your ministry area. Praying for your leader aligns your heart with God and helps you assume the best while extending grace. Don't let entitlement sneak in. Let your heart toward your leader overflow with gratitude.

> *"Make allowance for each other's faults, and forgive anyone who offends you. Remember, the Lord forgave you, so you must forgive others" Colossians 3:13 (NLT).*

You may have fallen into the trap of thinking your leader is there to serve you, but today, I want to remind you to honor and serve the Lord through serving your leader. God has placed you in this role, at this time, under this leader. Trust Him and serve from the overflow of your love for the Lord.

> *"Love each other with genuine affection, and take delight in honoring each other" Romans 12:10 (NLT).*

3 Questions to Ask Yourself

1. How can I align my work more closely with the principle of working as though working for the Lord?

2. How can I better anticipate and meet the needs of my leader this week?

3. Why is it essential for me to consistently demonstrate integrity and enthusiasm in my work?

First Step

What's your first step to initiate a conversation with your leader to understand their current priorities and challenges?

_____

_____

About Corey

Corey Jones is the Executive Pastor at Southern Hills in GA and strives to be an opportunist, learner, and helper. His mission is to help leaders take their next step in personal development. Find out more at:

CoreyRayJones.com

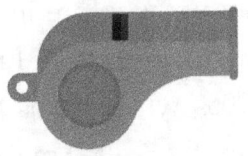

6
Hearing God's Voice
Jim Wideman

One of the biggest surprises for me since I've started coaching others is how many leaders have shared with me that they are not totally confident in their ability to hear the voice of God. How about you? Are you confident in your ability to hear God's voice?

This is a subject that I have covered with every age group I've ever worked with from kids to college. It was something that my wife and I taught our own kids and that we are now teaching our grands. It's also something that I've been intentional to help every single person I've coached to do better. Why is this so important? If a dog can know the voice of his master, how much more can we who are intelligent beings know the voice of our Master. I remember way back in the 1900s when I was a boy and my mom or grandmother called me to come in from play, I remember recognizing their voice and I would head home immediately from up the street. I've found that God's voice can always be trusted. When Jesus left this earth, He promised He would send us another comforter who would lead us into all things; in fact, Jesus said "it's better for you that I go away." God doesn't lead His kids into trouble. He'll never lead us some place weird or in the wrong direction. I've found over and over again "Thus says the Lord" always works!

When I call people on the phone I always tell them who I am, even though in most cases today, caller I.D. has already given me up. Most of the time the people I'm calling say, "I know who this is. I recognize your accent. I'd know your voice anywhere." Why? Because we are in relationship. If I can recognize the voice of those

I am in relationship with on earth, especially my kids and grands, I should be able to recognize the voice of Jesus, if I'm one of His kids.

One of my favorite chapters in the Bible is John 10. In the first five verses we find that Jesus is sharing an eternal truth with the Pharisees. Here Jesus lets us know He is our shepherd and we are His sheep. He says here that His sheep know His voice and they follow Him and that they won't recognize the voice of a stranger (the devil). This truth has been something I find myself saying almost every day since I've been walking with the Lord. "I am your sheep and you are my shepherd, I know your voice. The voice of a stranger I will not follow!"

Jim, are you saying you have heard God speak audibly? I personally have not, but I've heard Him speak in other ways. I do know people who have heard an audible voice. I remember when our daughter Yancy was little, she would come to her mom and I and say, "I heard you calling my name. What did you want?" At first, I would just tell her we didn't call her and she would run back to her room. In a few minutes she was back saying, "Dad, what did you want?" I then would tell her what Eli told the boy Samuel in 1 Samuel 3:1-10. I told her, if you hear it again say, "Speak, Lord, your servant is listening!" Sure enough, it was the Lord. This still happens with her to this day. I know God's presence and I hunger for it. I also know His voice when He speaks. His Word reveals how He speaks to others and we can learn from these examples how to expect to hear from Him.

Here are the five ways I practice and have coached others to hear God's voice.

1. Dive into the Bible

This is an easy step to follow. Just grab your Bible and dig into the Scriptures. The Bible is more than just an ordinary book; it's God speaking directly to you! The more you read, the more you'll recognize His voice. 2 Timothy 3:16-17 NIV says, "All Scripture is God-breathed and is useful for teaching, rebuking, correcting and training in righteousness, so that the servant of God may be thoroughly equipped for every good work." John 1:1-5 NIV, tells us, "In the beginning was the Word, and the Word was with God, and the Word was God. He was with God in the beginning. Through Him all things were made; without Him nothing was made that has been made. In Him was life, and that life was the light of all mankind …The Word became flesh and made His dwelling among us." If Jesus and the Word are the same, you can hear His voice through His Word. I have heard all my life that the Bible is the only book that when you are reading it, it is also reading you! God's Word is a light unto your path, a lamp unto your feet, and like a map, it guides your steps to direct your life in the way you should go.

2. Tune in through prayer

Think of prayer as a direct line to God, like having a personal chat with a friend. It's a two-way conversation where you can talk and listen. It seems like talking is becoming a lost form of communicating with friends. Since the Holy Spirit doesn't use text, don't panic. Just talk to Him and then listen. One of my favorite scriptures is 1 Thessalonians 5:16-18 (ESV) where it says, "Rejoice always, pray without ceasing, give thanks in all circumstances; for this is the will of God in Christ Jesus for you." Just like He speaks in multiple ways, I've found His answers also come in multiple ways. The question is: Are you listening?

3. Listen for the whisper

God often speaks through the still, small voice of the Holy Spirit. It's like having an internal guide nudging you in the right direction. This voice often leads, points out things, and provides guidance. Sometimes I have what I call a divine knowing. I don't know why I know this is the right thing to do. I just know that I need to obey it. Just like we taught Yancy and Eli taught

Samuel to learn to say, "Speak, Lord, for your servant is listening" sometimes God's guidance comes when you least expect it. Pay attention to the doors He opens and closes in your life. Remember, delays are often divine protection! I love Proverbs 6:3, especially the last part, "In all your ways, acknowledge Him, and He'll make your path straight.

4. Seek wisdom from trusted friends

God speaks through the wisdom of others. Experience is the best teacher, but it doesn't have to be your experience. Surround yourself with trusted advisers who can offer godly counsel and confirm what you're hearing. Proverbs 11:14 NIV says, "Where there is no counsel, the people fall; but in the multitude of counselors there is safety."

5. Watch for divine dreams and visions

God loves to communicate through dreams, visions, and pictures. Keep a journal by your bed to jot down any vivid dreams or impressions you receive. Acts 2:17 NIV, "In the last days, God says, 'I will pour out My Spirit on all people. Your sons and daughters will prophesy, your young men will see visions, your old men will dream dreams.'"

Hearing Jesus' voice doesn't require superpowers, just practice and patience. The more you listen, the clearer His voice becomes.

Jesus said, "His sheep recognize His voice." Let's get started and do some listening!

3 Questions to Ask Yourself

1. Are you setting aside time each day to hear God's voice?

2. Are you doing what He's already told you to do?

3. Have you given permission for God to speak to you and the Holy Spirit to guide you today?

First Step

What's your first step going to be to hear God's voice better?

_____

_____

About Jim

Jim Wideman has been helping ministry leaders thrive for a half century. He's currently The Executive Pastor of Ministries at Conduit Church in Franklin, Tennessee. He also offers group and individual coaching throughout the year and has authored over

15 books for NextGen ministry. Find out more about his resources and coaching at:
jimwideman.com

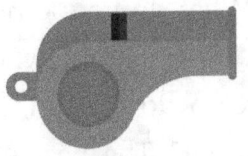

7
Empowering Volunteers
Andrea Goslee

Everyone wants more volunteer leaders for their ministry—not just any volunteer, but reliable, spirit-filled, high-level leaders you can count on to help you raise up the next generation. What if I told you there are five action steps you can take now to help you find, develop, and raise up volunteers to lead at the next level? These leaders are already in your ministry, just waiting to be asked, identified, and empowered to use the gifts God has given them.

1. Get to know each volunteer personally to assess their potential

Think about everyone on your current volunteer team. What do you know about them? Do you know their family, where they work, what they like to do for fun, and even their favorite restaurant? The best way to identify leaders who can lead at the next level is to get to know the people already within your care. Show them you care about them by taking an interest in their life outside their serving role. Help them realize their potential by calling out specific gifts you see in them to lead.

Some simple ways to get to know your volunteers and assess their potential include:

- Create a favorites card to find out their interests
- Host a game night, cook-out, or fun event
- Schedule a block of time to meet volunteers at a local coffee shop and invite them to drop in for a free coffee
- Find ways to serve together as a volunteer team

- Attend activities volunteers are involved in

Spending time with volunteers outside of church will help you identify their strengths, interests, and potential.

2. Create roles with job descriptions where you want to add leadership

When I served in a start-up church, I made a weekly Walmart run, filling up a cart with activity supplies that might include balloons for games, Cheerios for babies, or 10-12 cans of whipped cream. The person at the checkout always commented, "Are you having a party?" or, "You must really like whipped cream!" I enjoyed shopping for supplies, but it took away a chunk of time I could have spent connecting with people. That gave me an idea! What if I created a volunteer role for someone to do the shopping?

From that moment, I created a simple job description, and each week, I sent a list of items to a mom who would shop for supplies, drop them off, and sometimes even stay to divide them into groups for the Sunday experience. As I built a relationship with this volunteer, I discovered she loved to cook. This led to another volunteer role as the Kids Ministry Caterer. Through this new role, she began preparing all the food for our volunteer leader events. The food was spectacular, and she could use her gifts to serve others.

Think about places where you want to grow or expand your ministry. Do you need a "hype" person to greet families as they come down the hallway? … a communication champion who can take your social media to the next level? … or an events person extraordinaire who will take the lead on your next big idea? You can create any role that will benefit your ministry and free up your time to do the things only you can do.

3. Identify character and spiritual depth

One of the most important things to consider when elevating leaders to the next level is to know their character and their spiritual depth. Many people can be competent, but the God-chosen person to lead at the next level should have excellent character and be connected to Jesus. You want volunteers leading in your ministry who are led by the Holy Spirit, guiding them as they make decisions and lead.

How do you find the right people? First, pray! Ask God to show you who He wants to elevate to a new leadership position. Next, find out if they are in a small group, tithing, and attending church regularly. If possible, find additional ways to gain an understanding of their spiritual depth through activities like prayer, Bible studies, or an online devotional.

4. Provide growth opportunities

If you plant a vegetable garden, it will grow best when you faithfully water the plants and till the soil. It's the same with volunteer leaders. You need to develop them and provide opportunities to grow into the next-level leader that God designed them to be.

One of the best ways to lead a volunteer to the next level is 1-on-1 mentoring. Depending on the size of your ministry, you may be the best person to do this. For others, you may have a team of faithful leaders you've already developed who can pour into and develop their leadership and faith skills.

You can also create a leadership pipeline. This is a progressive and intentional system that you want volunteers to flow through before becoming a leader. This could include weekly gatherings, book studies, or a higher-intensity training program to develop their leadership skills.

Above all, invite them on the journey with you. Jesus said, "Come follow Me." He didn't just tell His disciples what to do. It wasn't until after they had spent time following Him and being with Him that He sent them out to lead on their own. Invite volunteers to lead alongside you. Let them see your heart and why you do things the way you do.

5. Clarify authority and delegate ownership

Once you've identified and developed leaders, it's important to clarify their level of authority.

- What decisions will they make on their own?
- What do you want them to check with you for input?

You want to delegate ownership to them, but only after walking through the expectations in advance.

I hosted an all-church lemonade stand for kids to raise money for a global mission. One of my volunteers was passionate about the mission, so I asked her to lead the event. We met together, talked through the specifics of the event, decided what she could do on her own, and clarified what she should check with me before moving forward. She had complete authority on decorating the booth and recruiting volunteers. After she found the supplies, I approved the budget before purchasing. After working through the process, she was able to take over more responsibility the following year. It was a win for her and the ministry!

3 Questions to Ask Yourself

1. How much time are you spending with people outside your weekly service times?

2. What leadership roles could you add to enhance your current ministry?

3. What growth opportunities can you provide to help volunteers grow in their leadership?

First Step

What is one action step you can take to raise up and empower a volunteer to lead at the next level?

_____

_____

About Andrea

Andrea Goslee is the Central Kids Director at Rock City Church in Columbus, OH, raising up the next generation of leaders. She is part of the First Look writing team for Orange and the author of the *Baptism Adventure* series that resources parents to help kids take the next steps in their faith. You can connect with her at:

andreagoslee7@gmail.com

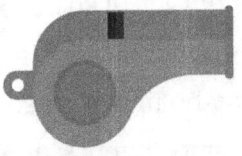

8
Asking Better Questions
Jim Wideman

If you know me, you know that I value questions. In fact, I don't just value them—I absolutely love questions. I've never encountered a question I didn't like.

Questions are powerful tools that stimulate thinking, evaluation, and growth. They are the catalysts for learning and the first step toward change. Something I learned in college from my favorite professor, Dr. Phillip Stanberry, is, "A questioning faith is a growing faith, and there's a crucial distinction between doubt and genuine inquiry." I've found the best way to learn something every day is to ask questions every day!

1. Don't let fear rob you of an opportunity to learn

There is no such thing as a dumb question. While there may be uninformed answers, every question has value. Even seemingly simple or obvious questions can lead to profound insights. The key is asking the right people the right questions, as this opens doors to wisdom and understanding. Proverbs 4:6-8 emphasizes the value of wisdom, urging you to seek and embrace it because it protects, exalts, and honors you.

One of the most effective ways to grow is by learning from others, especially those in leadership. Whenever you have the opportunity to be with another leader, prepare questions in advance. Prioritize them in case time is limited. Seek out learning opportunities through networking, websites, forums, podcasts, and blogs. Even if you're shy, don't let fear rob you of an opportunity to learn.

2. Seek out learning opportunities

Don't wait for learning opportunities to come to you; seek out others you want to learn from. Phone appointments and emails can be valuable tools for learning. When making a phone appointment, clearly state the subject or purpose and send your questions ahead of time. Regularly email questions to those you want to learn from, but limit them to no more than two per month. Use multiple-choice questions for those who know you well and reserve complex questions for live communication. Additionally, take advantage of Q&A opportunities, comment lines, and even other people's questions. Group coaching is particularly beneficial, because you learn from the questions of others as well as your own.

3. Use questions to locate and understand

Questions are a good way to locate what and where people you are leading are thinking. In Matthew 16:13-18, you find one of the most profound moments in the New Testament. Jesus, in the region of Caesarea Philippi, asked His disciples, "Who do people say the Son of Man is?" They replied with various names: John the Baptist, Elijah, Jeremiah, or one of the prophets. But then Jesus asked them directly, "But what about you? Who do you say I am?" Simon Peter answered, "You are the Christ, the Son of the living God." Jesus affirmed Peter's answer, acknowledging that this revelation came not from man but from His Father in heaven. This passage underscores the power and significance of asking the right questions. It turned a casual conversation into a masterclass and a life-changing moment.

Jesus exemplified the art of asking questions throughout His life and ministry. From a young age, He engaged with teachers in the temple, listening and asking questions that amazed those who heard Him (Luke 2:46-52). His questions were not just for the sake of inquiry; they were strategic, and designed to teach, provoke thought, and encourage spiritual growth.

In His ministry, Jesus used questions in various ways. He asked questions to teach or make a point, to locate people spiritually, and to get them to think and evaluate their lives. He also used questions to encourage change and deepen understanding.

4. Plan and prepare your questions before you ask

To maximize the benefits of asking questions, focus on those that help you learn and understand more deeply. Ask questions that promote thought, help you evaluate yourself and your thinking, and encourage growth. Use questions to locate others, compare perspectives, confirm ideas, and encourage further questioning.

Here are some of my favorite questions that can lead to significant insights.

- What would you do differently?
- What are you reading, and why is it important?

- Where do you get your ideas? What or who inspires you?
- What trends, gauges, and statistics do you watch, both for the present and the future?
- What is the secret to your success?
- Can you share any significant keys or principles you've learned?
- What habits contribute to your study, friendships, stress management, and parenting?

Asking about procedures, gadgets, tools, methods, techniques, and tricks can also be incredibly enlightening. Understanding the "why" behind actions and decisions is often more important than knowing "what" was done.

5. Ask as many questions as possible

The more questions you ask, the more you learn, and the better you become at asking insightful questions. It's essential to start with questions for yourself before seeking answers from others. Reflect on what God has been saying to you and what He wants to communicate. Consider what you have been learning about yourself, your marriage, your family, and your ministry. Evaluate your past, present, and future, and think about the leaders, kids, and parents in your life.

Identify what you need to stop doing and what you should continue. Assess which systems need strengthening or establishing, and consider whether your thinking needs to change. Reflect on who you are mentoring and who is mentoring you. Consider what you have stopped doing that you need to start again. Finally, evaluate how you are spending your time.

Asking the right questions is a powerful practice that can transform your personal and spiritual growth. Jesus demonstrated the importance of questions in His ministry, and you can follow His example by using questions to learn, grow, and change. Whether it's in personal reflection, learning from others, or engaging with Scripture, the right questions can lead to profound insights and deeper understanding. As you cultivate the habit of asking thoughtful questions, you'll find yourself continually growing in wisdom and knowledge. Remember, there are no dumb questions—only opportunities for learning and growth.

3 Questions to Ask Yourself

1. Who has God put in your life that you could be learning from but are not taking advantage of?

2. Who would you like to learn from? Make a list, prepare questions you would like to ask them, and schedule time to reach out throughout the year.

3. What questions should you be asking those you are leading to help them be more effective and promote growth?

Next Step

What's your first step to up your question game and ask better questions?

_____

_____

About Jim

Jim Wideman has been helping ministry leaders thrive for a half century. He's currently The Executive Pastor of Ministries at Conduit Church in Franklin, Tennessee. He also offers group and individual coaching throughout the year and has authored over 15 books for NextGen ministry. Find out more about his resources and coaching at:

jimwideman.com

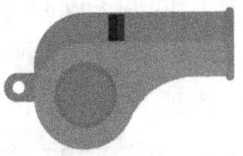

9
Managing Leadership Transitions
Rachel Pilcher

When I dreamed of being in church ministry I never thought I would be headed into a season with my seventh lead pastor. I've served at three different churches in the last fourteen years and I have had the privilege of serving under six different leaders (the seventh starts later this year). I jokingly say now, "If I join your staff, you better be ready for some transition." It seems to be a mantle that I wear. In the Old and New Testaments you see transitions of leadership, from Elijah to Elisha, Moses to Joshua, John the Baptist to Jesus, and Jesus to the Disciples. Each of these biblical transitions model how you can be ready for a modern-day transition.

1. Honor always

One of the most important things you can do as a leader is honor always. Whether you are the one transitioning, or your leader is transitioning, always lead with honor. When in ministry, you have differences of preferences, ministry styles, and sometimes even theology. During transition, all of those ideas need to be put aside and only honor should be offered. When you have a leader who you value as a pastor, mentor, and friend, honor comes easily. However, when you have a Saul rather than a David, it can be much harder to honor. Just remember the Lord anointed Saul just as much as He anointed David. You are to ask to live a life that honors God-chosen leadership. When new leadership is added, be supportive, and remember that to honor new leadership is not to hurt or damage past leadership success. A dear friend, Gail Starnes, once told me that you could be the difference in (the new pastor's) success. Be present with them, honor always. You will likely have to be a role model for your church people to honor new leadership as well. People will watch you and follow your lead of honor.

2. Embrace change with joy

When new leadership is added to your team, whether from a lead pastor position or another staff member, know that their experiences and passions will bring change to your team. I've always heard that change can be scary, but change means you are growing and adapting.

During one staff transition, we added a new person to the team. I noticed quickly that they had a lot of the same passions and giftings as I did. When they came on the team, I could have easily been threatened or territorial; however, when I embraced the change with joy, I realized the Lord sent me a helper and a dear friend! So many memories were made during our season together and we are still dear friends today.

3. Remember the "why"

What is the "why" of church? People!… for people to find Jesus and experience a life-changing relationship with Him. As you go through transition, you need to remember PEOPLE. When changes are coming, or decisions are near, remember people. Talk to people, see the people. During transition, you should spend 25% more time with people. People will feel disconnected during transition, especially if the lead pastor is transitioning. It will be easy to miss services and think that no one will notice. Be the person who notices. Reach out to more people during transitions, to ensure they feel connected.

4. Keep your job description up to date

This one is fully practical. Whenever a leader has transitioned to our team, I get asked, "What exactly do you do?" It's easy to say, "Well, I'm the kids' pastor." But, if you have worked on a ministry team longer than a minute you know we all do things that aren't on our job description. Keeping a list of current responsibilities is extremely helpful when a transition is happening. I have gone so far as to keep a list of what everyone does, so that we can help transition quickly and faster in that one area. New lead pastors have loved this and it has been so helpful when they want to change or find some alignment with staff. It also cuts down on "figure it out" time for them and we can start to work together faster.

5. Start and leave well

If you are the one transitioning, start and leave well. When runners have to pass the baton, they actually practice it during the season. If we cannot pass the baton well, transition will fall flat.

Starting well: Build relationships by spending a lot of quality time with people. Do things together outside of church. It's easy to spend a lot of time with your leaders, but also pull in your ministry-focused people (parents, kids, youth, etc.) Invite people to your home, out to lunch after church on Sunday, and begin doing life together. Dream together, look towards the future, and celebrate the past together. As a leader who can celebrate past leadership and past seasons, this will really cement you to the team and the church. My rule of thumb is do nothing but observe and pray for the first 90 days. After 90 days you can start dreaming and sharing the vision with key leaders for the next year. After 120 days you can start shifting the most important things. I make a list of things that need to be shifted and updated into three categories. These categories are divided by three colors:

- **Red**: Things that need attention and solutions in the next 30 days.
- **Yellow**: Things that need attention and solutions in the next 60 days.
- **Green**: Things that need attention and solutions in the next 90-120 days.

These categories help me stay focused and

get things accomplished instead of being overwhelmed. This also helps me track my progress and report well to a new lead pastor.

Leaving Well: If it is your time to transition to a new opportunity, the best thing you can do is leave well. If you have a good relationship with your lead pastor (or direct report), make sure they know early on that transition is coming. Try hard to not let them be surprised by transition news. The best thing a leader can say to you is, "Yea, I felt the transition coming too." After speaking to your leader, make a list together of the items they would like you to complete before your end date. Then, work hard to complete it. Spend time encouraging your team to stay involved and engaged in the interim. Think about what the team will need while you aren't there. Make sure to leave all of your files and passwords that people may need when you leave. Leave the door open for contact from your leadership and team. It's an honor that many of the past leaders I served with continue to contact me for coaching, resources, and help when needed.

Transitions in ministry are inevitable and how you manage them are key to the church and your success in ministry. We, as the church, haven't had a great track record with transitions, so this is an area we can all do better in! Commit the process to prayer, fasting, and coaching, and it will work so much better than it has in the past.

3 Questions to Ask Yourself

1. Are you in a season of transition right now? Are you sensing one coming? Do you know of someone in transition?

2. Who is someone on your team who you need to honor this week?

3. Pull out your job description list and see if it is up to date. Work on getting it more inclusive this week.

First Step

What is your first step to manage a transition you're facing?

_____

_____

About Rachel

Rachel Pilcher has been leading in kids' ministry and NextGEN ministry since 2010. She is the NextGEN Pastor at Griffin First Assembly in Griffin, GA. Rachel grew up in church as a pastor's kid. She loves coaching the next generation of students and leaders to find their full potential in Jesus and answer the call on their lives. She is married to Michael, a police investigator, and they have a daughter, Elyn. You can contact Rachel at:

RachelPilcher@gmail.com

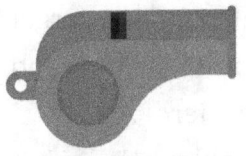

10
Helping Your Own Kids Love Jesus and His Church
Jim Wideman

Raising kids who love Jesus and the church is a high calling, especially for those of us in ministry. It's about creating a home environment that prioritizes faith and family, not just the church. Here are five practical and fun things my wife and I did that you can do to help your kids grow up loving Jesus and His church.

1. Prioritize your home over the church

Yes, I know, what happens at church feels incredibly important. But let's not forget that what happens at home is even more important. Sometimes, ministry families get so wrapped up in church life that they forget to nurture their home life. I am first a husband, second a dad, and third a minister.

Keep a healthy balance between home and ministry. The idea that "I'll take care of God's house, and He'll take care of mine" isn't biblical. We need to be intentional about making our homes a place where our kids can grow in their faith. Watch how many nights you allow the church to have. In a perfect world, my goal is no more than two. My wife gets one and my family get the other four. Also, give your phone a bedtime. Just because many of us use a cell phone for both our work and home number doesn't mean you are available to work 24/7. Remember, even convicts get time off for good behavior.

Joshua 24:15 (NKJV) says, "But as for me and my house, we will serve the Lord." Make sure your home is a place where serving the Lord is a priority. I have seen with my kids and now with their kids, faith is often more caught than taught. Let them hear you quoting God's

Word on a continuous basis.

Fun Tip: Have a weekly family night where church talk is off-limits. Jesus talk is encouraged. There's a big difference in the two. Play games, watch movies, or do something everyone loves. This helps to create a balance and show your kids that home is a sanctuary of love and faith.

2. Spend quality time with your kids

Let's face it, ministry can be all-consuming. But spending quality time with your kids can make a huge difference in their faith journey.

Make time for your kids by adding them to your calendar. Even though my kids are grown, I still prioritize my relationship with them as well as with my grands. Here's how.

Daily I send a text or give them a call. A quick chat can go a long way. I've started sending a text to my grands now that the oldest has a phone. I send a simple thought, prayer, or "I love you." This works with extended family also. My great niece is off to college and I've begun to message her, as well as comment on my family's social media posts.

Weekly, I try to still have dates with my kids and grands, family outings (we are a Putt-Putt family), and even include them in our errands. Make it fun. My youngest grand loves to go to Costco with us to test the samples.

We include our grown kids on vacations, special trips, and events they enjoy. Let them be involved in planning too. The key is to remember to be present at all times! Ephesians 5:15-17 reminds us to make the most of every opportunity because the days are evil. Make spending time with your kids a lifestyle choice.

Fun Tip: Think of each person in your family. Be intentional about recurring events you can schedule A breakfast, a lunch, a weekly field trip, cooking classes, or art time. Google day trips and community classes and activities in your area. Make it a regular part of your week.

3. Involve your family in ministry

Including your family in ministry helps them see the honor in being called and prevents negative feelings toward the church. Maintain a positive attitude always! Philippians 2:14-15 (NLT) advises us to do everything without complaining so we can shine brightly. Avoid speaking negatively about the church or its people. Make your kids feel involved and valued in the ministry. Emphasize the positive aspects of serving God together.

Fun Tip: Let your kids take on a "mini-ministry" role that matches their interests. Maybe they can help with tech, greet people, or even assist in children's ministry. Make it a family affair!

4. Be consistent and fair in discipline

Consistency in discipline helps your children understand boundaries and expectations without feeling burdened by unrealistic demands. Let the punishment fit the crime and remember what it's like to be their age. Don't impose unrealistic expectations on them because you are employed by a church!

Fun Tip: Create a "family court" where everyone gets to discuss rules and consequences together. It makes discipline a learning experience and insures everyone feels heard.

5. Foster open communication and inclusion

Keeping lines of communication open with your children helps them feel valued and understood. My wife and I always tried to maintain an open door policy. Establish an environment where your kids feel comfortable talking to you about anything. How?

Honesty always! Share your own mistakes and temptations. Be open about your experiences. Try to listen actively. Don't overreact when they express different or wrong views. Use these moments to teach them what the Bible says. Include your kids in family prayer and decision-making as they grow. This teaches them the importance of seeking God together as a family.

Fun Tip: Have regular "family meetings" where everyone gets to share their thoughts and ideas. It can be about anything from what movie to watch on family night to discussing deeper faith questions.

Raising kids who love Jesus and the church involves a balanced approach where home life and ministry complement each other. By prioritizing your home, spending quality time together, involving your family in ministry, being fair in discipline, and fostering open communication, you can help your children develop a strong and lasting faith.

Remember, it's not about perfection but about making consistent efforts to show your kids that loving Jesus and His church can be a joyful, everyday part of life.

3 Questions to Ask Yourself

1. Which one of these 5 things jump out at you the most that you need to start working on immediately?

2. Is there something you need to ask your family's forgiveness for that you need to stop doing?

3. Right now do you feel like you are married to the church and dating your family? Or are you married to your family and dating your church?

First Step

What will be your first step in making the corrections needed for your kids to not resent Jesus and His Church?

_____

_____

About Jim

Jim Wideman has been helping ministry leaders thrive for a half century. He's currently The Executive Pastor of Ministries at Conduit Church in Franklin, Tennessee. He also offers group and individual coaching throughout the year and has authored over 15 books for NextGen ministry. Find out more about his resources and coaching at:

jimwideman.com

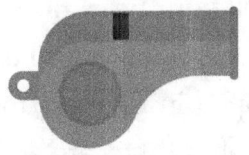

11
Caring for Your Heart
Vicki Abbott

Can we talk about caring for your heart in ministry? No one here probably went to medical school, but you might remember from biology class that your heart is a muscle. You might also remember from biology or gym class that muscles take work to keep in shape. Getting muscles in shape and keeping them strong is why bodybuilders spend so much time in the gym and fitness competitors watch everything they eat. Now you might be thinking, I'm reading this book about ministry, so why are you talking about my heart?

Your heart reacts when you are exercising and when you are stressed. Have you ever been startled and felt your heart race from being surprised? Everyone, right? Your heart reacts when situations happen in ministry too. You need to take initiative about the care and attention you give your heart to anticipate those surprises.

In a study by Barna (2022) research, it states that on average 38% of pastors considered quitting the ministry within the last year. Could this be prevented? I believe so. Here are five helpful steps to get you on your way.

1. Go vertical first

Spending time with God needs to be the number one priority in keeping your heart healthy in ministry. Your relationship with Him as His child is the most important thing you can do. Spending time in prayer and going to the Holy Spirit for guidance is where you need to start. Your vertical relationship needs to be healthy for all other horizontal relationships to follow in a healthy way.

Your relationship includes spending time in prayer, asking for guidance, and getting His direction for your ministry. Is your heart bitter against anything? What do you need to have a chat with Jesus about? What does your heart need to be softened to? Start by going vertical and spending time with Him.

There was a season when I was feeling burned out. It was a hotel room while at a ministry conference that became a sacred space where I would fall more in love with Jesus than I had ever been. It was in that room that the Holy Spirit spoke to me. He reminded me of my call, and more importantly, of my relationship with Him. It was also there that I was reminded of the importance of being in the Word.

2. Spend time in the Word

Do you have a life verse or a verse that roots you in your calling to ministry? You may not, so that might be a step you take after reading this chapter. If you do, do you lean on that scripture?

For me, it is Philippians 4:13 (NLT), "For I can do everything through Christ, who gives me strength." It is the reminder of His call on my life and that He is the One who gives me what I need. In the Bible, you read that Paul learned to be content in all circumstances because of his reliance on his Heavenly Father.

You should be spending time in the Word daily. It is also helpful to be part of a Bible study or a community group where you can grow and learn from one another. God's Word is our instruction book and should be where we spend time learning, growing, and becoming more like Him.

3. Don't do ministry alone

Do not do ministry alone! I cannot say this enough. If you are at a small church, reach out to someone in ministry in your city, join a ministry community, or work with a coach. If you are at a medium or large church, ministry can still be lonely. Find connections outside of your church with like-minded ministry leaders. I know I have a group of people who I have continually met with for over four years from all different areas of the United States, and I believe it has made us all better ministry leaders.

You should find people who are ahead of you in ministry and learn from them. You should also find people who are newer to ministry and still have a fire and passion to learn. Pour into them. Those leaders have a way of bringing a fresh perspective. Doing ministry together can help protect your heart against bitterness, loneliness, and against comparison of other ministry leaders and churches.

4. Set good boundaries

Your heart matters to your personal and ministry work, and you should have boundaries for both. You are called to ministry and to your family. Make sure you have an excellent work schedule and then make time for your family.

Your heart needs rest for longevity in ministry and it is okay to be unavailable on your days off. Everyone needs a Sabbath and you should make sure to take one each week. God rested on day seven and you need to as well. Sundays are often not a Sabbath because of ministry work. Do you have a Sabbath? If not, you may need to make that a priority for your heart.

Get into service. This can be hard when you are short on volunteers. Does your church have an online option or an early morning rehearsal where you can listen to worship to set your heart in the right place? Lead yourself well, so you are healthy to lead others and from a full heart.

5. Remember why you were called to ministry!

In ministry there are going to be different seasons. Ecclesiastes 3:1 (NLT) says, "For everything there is a season, a time for every activity under heaven." There are going to be seasons when ministry is fun and seasons that are hard and stressful. No matter what you do, there are going to be times when you are short-staffed, going through a leadership challenge, or limited with volunteers. It can be easy for you to want to walk away in those seasons, so it is important for you to remember your "why" in ministry.

Do you remember the first time someone talked to you about Jesus or when you committed your life to following Christ?

I have been in ministry for over 22 years and it has not been easy. Longevity in ministry is hard and takes work. It can be easier to walk away than to turn your heart inward and find the root cause for wanting to leave. Guarding your heart now may help so when the trials come, you will have the tools to notice it and work through it. The starting place for caring for your heart is to spend time on a regular basis in quiet reflection to evaluate where your heart is. Put a recurring appointment on your calendar and use that time intentionally to access your heart.

3 Questions to Ask Yourself

1. What strategy can you have in place to stay connected to Jesus?

2. What are five truths you can remember when things are hard? Write them down and place them in a spot where you will frequently see them.

3. Who do you have to reach out to who will pray with you, who will talk about the tough times in ministry, and who will keep you accountable to your calling?

First Step

What will be your first step to care for your heart?

_____

_____

About Vicki

Vicki Abbott has been serving in children's ministry for 23 years and currently serves at Ada Bible, a multi-site church in Grand Rapids, Michigan, as the Director of Children's Ministry. She is passionate about leadership development and enjoys collaborating with others. Vicki has a heart for helping leaders discern their calling and achieve longevity in ministry. Her favorite volunteer role is serving as a large group storyteller, and she especially loves speaking at camp and has been on the speaker team at CPC as well as serving as a ministry coach for multi-site leaders. Vicki loves shoes that sparkle, confetti, and believes there is always a reason to celebrate. Contact Vicki at:

abbottvl@gmail.com

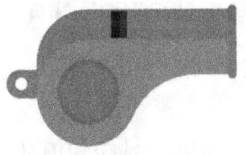

12
There's No Junior Holy Spirit
Jim Wideman

No matter your church background or denomination, the Holy Spirit wants to be a part of your church to help you reach the next generation and empower you to successfully make Jesus known to all. Acts 1:8 (NIV) says, "You shall receive power when the Holy Spirit comes on you." We all need His power and help.

There isn't a different Holy Spirit for children and another one for adults. That's what I mean when I say, "There's no Junior Holy Spirit!" Romans 8:11 (NIV) tells us, "He's the same Holy Spirit that raised Christ Jesus from the dead and He lives in us!" Here are five things I cover when

I coach NextGen leaders about including the Holy Spirit in their ministry.

1. Make Him known

What do kids need to know about the Holy Spirit? Start at the beginning: He was sent by Jesus to be our helper. We all need help! Kids also need to know He's the third person of the Godhead. That's pretty important. Yet, in many churches, He's not talked about much, He's underutilized, and He's somewhat devalued.

Do I talk to preschoolers about the Trinity? No, but I sure explain it to elementary kids.

We serve a triune God! Each part is important. Being from Alabama, football is a big deal. I learned at an early age that the game has three parts: Offense, Defense, and Special Teams. Jesus is our Offense; you can't score in life without Him. Father God is our Defense; He's our protector. The Holy Spirit is our Special Teams. Without all three, you'll never achieve all Father God has for you.

Acts 2:17-18 (NIV) tells us, "In the last days, God says, I will pour out my Spirit on all people. Your sons and daughters will prophesy, your young men will see visions, your old men will dream dreams. Even on my servants, both men and women, I will pour out my Spirit in those days, and they will prophesy." In the last days' move of the Spirit, the first group that's mentioned are the sons and daughters. Kids don't just need to know who the Holy Spirit is, but they also need to know what He does and why. Sadly, most curriculums don't mention the Holy Spirit at all, so it's up to you to include Him!

2. You get what you make room for

Stephen Covey wrote a great book years ago entitled *7 Habits of Effective People*. The first habit is the best one in my opinion: "Start with the end in mind." What are you aiming for? Encounter, presence, anointing, or revival? If these words are foreign to you, look them up. They are biblical!

In Matthew 19:14 (NIV), Jesus said, "Let the little children come to me and do not hinder them." Child development is not equal to supernatural development. Church is not supposed to look like school. The problem with school is it's not experiential or hands-on. I believe church should be a place where you do more than learn about the Holy Spirit; you should experience Him as well. "Encounter" means to come face to face with. Encounter is something you must cultivate! What is kids' church and why does it matter? It should be a training ground to experience and understand church. It's different from large group and small group.

We all know Proverbs 22:6 by heart: "Train up a child in the way they should go, and when they are old they won't depart." Training is a whole lot more than verbal instruction. Every child should understand these essential truths no matter what curriculum you use.

- We were made by Father God in His image. (We are all Image Bearers.)

- Jesus is the only way to be saved.
- The Bible is God's Word.
- We were made to worship.
- The Holy Spirit is our helper and our power source.

3. Welcome the Holy Spirit

Talk about Him from the start of class to the finish. Acknowledge Him to the kids. Point out His presence to the children. Introduce kids to the anointing. Teach about Him. Just like I mentioned above, kids need to know who the Holy Spirit is and what He does. It's up to you to involve and include Him.

Another important thing is to allow time to listen to Him. Kids can hear God's voice now. (See Chapter 6 about Hearing God's Voice.) Allow time for Him to show up. Include it in your lesson plan. Be sensitive to His leading. Be dependent on the Spirit rather than dependent on the lesson plan. Who's the boss? The Holy Spirit or the curriculum company?

4. Worship like David did

Be sure to read Chapter 16 by Yancy about making worship better. Worship is so much more than just singing songs, doing some motions, and throwing in some flashy dance moves. If you haven't read Yancy's book, *Sweet Sound: The Power of Discipling Kids in Worship*, be sure to order a copy at YancyMinistries.com/sweet-sound.

We were made to worship God! The Bible tells us that God inhabits the praises of His people. If you want God's presence in kids' church, teach kids what true worship is and how to press into God's presence. They will follow the adults' lead. Teach kids biblical responses and worship postures: lifting our hands, clapping our hands, kneeling, dancing, bowing down, verbally praising Him, singing, and even being silent before Him.

5. Practice makes perfect

When I started in kidmin, there was nothing to buy or models to follow. Looking back, that wasn't a bad thing; it was one of the best things, because it caused me to seek Jesus and ask Him what He wanted me to do. It caused me to develop my own strategy for my ministry. You can too!

Kids' church is the perfect place to safely practice and learn about the supernatural power of the Holy Spirit. If not at church, where? Kids aren't too small to practice hearing God's voice for themselves and for each other.

Where do I start? Teach kids every Bible story that mentions the person and work of the Holy Spirit (start at Jesus' birth). There are 563 verses in the Bible that mention the Holy Spirit. Kids need to not only know the Holy Spirit's purpose; they need to see Him in action. Kids need to be full of the Spirit. Why? Because the Bible says to! Whatever you are full of comes out when you are shaken. Kids need to know and experience the gifts of the Spirit as well as the fruit of the Spirit:

- Gifts: increased faith, healing, miracles, prophecy, word of knowledge, word of wisdom, the discernment of spirits, different kinds of tongues, and interpretation of tongues.
- Fruit: love, joy, peace, patience, kindness, goodness, faithfulness, gentleness, and self-control.

Teach kids they CAN walk in the supernatural NOW. Don't shortchange them or their encounters. Teach them to pray for one another. Allow time in the service for kids to see visions and hear God's voice. They are not too young to walk in the prophetic.

Tell kids stories of how the Holy Spirit worked in the lives of others, including their parents and grandparents. Building a great team is just as important as having great lessons. Kids' pastors must disciple the team as well as the kids. It starts with you, leader! You can't lead kids to a place you haven't been yourself.

Recognizing that there is no junior Holy Spirit is crucial for empowering children in their faith. By integrating these principles into your children's ministry, you create a vibrant and dynamic environment where young believers can experience the Holy Spirit's power and guidance, just as adults do. Let's nurture and celebrate the work of the Holy Spirit in every age group, starting with the youngest in your congregation. Through creative prayer activities, dynamic worship, engaging teachings, and hands-on experiences, your children's ministry will become a place where the Holy Spirit is not just talked about but experienced in real and powerful ways.

3 Questions to Ask Yourself

1. How can I make the Holy Spirit known to children in a relatable way?

2. Am I creating space for the Holy Spirit to move in our ministry?

3. Am I equipping children to walk in the supernatural power of the Holy Spirit?

First Step

What's the first step you'll take to teach kids there is no junior Holy Spirit?

_____

_____

About Jim

Jim Wideman has been helping ministry leaders thrive for a half century. He's currently The Executive Pastor of Ministries at Conduit Church in Franklin, Tennessee. He also offers group and individual coaching throughout the year and has authored over 15 books for NextGen ministry. Find out more about his resources and coaching at:

jimwideman.com

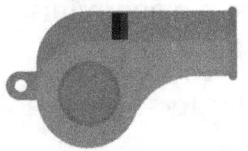

13
Small Church, Big Impact
Jeffrey Hunter

In 25+ years of ministry, I have learned a few things that helped me be successful in church ministry. These principles are usable in any size church, but my experience comes from being on staff at churches that were smaller in size but big in impact. In each ministry role, I saw the churches grow numerically and spiritually. The five principles I'm about to share in this chapter have served me well in every ministry I've overseen.

What are these magical principles? Well, they aren't magic at all really. They are concepts I learned from conference speakers, mentors, and a ministry coach. I saw the most growth in my own leadership and ministry when I had a coach.

Here are the top 5 things I've learned.

1. Alignment

You need to know your lead pastor's vision. More importantly, you must be able to support that vision. Here are some ways you can make sure you are aligned with your pastor's heart and vision for the church.

Spend time with your pastor and ask questions about their vision for the church. Their answers will shed light on what you need to focus on in ministry.

Actually listen to your pastor's sermons. Attend main service when possible, but on the weeks you can't attend, go back and watch the video of the service. Their messages will more than likely contain their vision.

You are an extension and representative of your pastor. The people who serve under you will follow your lead. Always maintain a supportive attitude of your pastor. (Romans 13:1 NLT "Everyone must submit to governing authorities. For all authority comes from God, and those in positions of authority have been placed there by God.")

2. Evaluation

It's important to evaluate every area of your ministry and do it often. Here's how I evaluate ministry:

Start by listing every area of ministry you oversee. Kids' pastors in smaller churches often oversee many areas of ministry and it can quickly become too much to handle if you are not prepared. The first step in evaluation is knowing what you are responsible for.

Break your ministry down further by listing the events, trainings, communication needs, and budgets for each of those areas that will also need to be evaluated.

3. Identify

Once you have made the evaluation lists, its time to identify which areas of ministry must be addressed first and prioritize them.

For example: areas of ministry high on your priority list might be weekend services, building a solid volunteer team, and creating an engaging follow-up plan.

List your tasks and put them into categories. A good method I recommend using to prioritize your tasks is the Eisenhower Matrix.

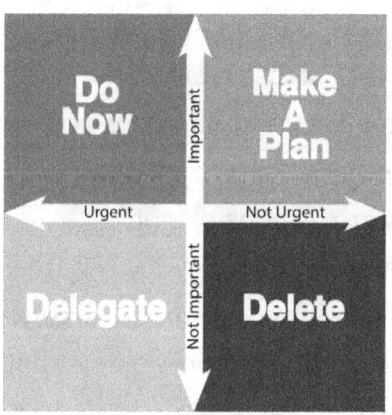

Identify tasks you can delegate to others and prioritize the tasks that only you can do on your own time. You may even find out you are doing some tasks that can be removed from your list altogether.

Tasks that fall in the important/urgent category should be prioritized at the top of your list.

Put all future tasks on your calendar, and set reminders.

4. Relationships

Identify current and potential volunteers in your church and begin to build relationships with them.

Always be on the lookout for people in your church who may be a good fit for your team. Out of all the ministries of the church, you most likely have the widest variety of roles and opportunities for people to serve in.

Go back to the lists you made during the "evaluation" step and take a look at your areas of ministry. Take the time to pray and ask God to lead you to the right people who will serve in each of those areas.

As you identify who may be a good fit, take the time to get to know them. Take them out for coffee or share a meal with them. If you are meeting with the opposite sex, I would suggest meeting in a public place or at the church office during office hours to keep everyone above reproach. Your time may be limited, but it will always be worth the time-investment to build relationships with the people, even if they don't end up serving in your ministry.

People enjoy serving alongside friends. Encourage your team to invite their friends and families to serve with them. I'm a big believer in spouses serving together. After all, Jesus sent His followers out two by two to do His ministry (Mark 6:7-13).

5. Processes

It's important to create processes for ministry with a growth mindset.

One of the things Jim taught me through his coaching was the importance of processes that will help you grow ministry, not just maintain it.

You need to evaluate where you are, decide where you want to go, then make a plan that will ideally get you there.

I have done this for several areas that used to overwhelm me, like recruiting volunteers. I used to be so frustrated when I took people through the spiritual gifts' test, and there was nothing specific about kids' ministry in the results. I finally realized that kids' ministry needs people from every gifting. That changed the process I had in place for recruiting.

I have never worked at a church large enough to hire an administrative assistant for kids' ministry. One day, I met a young lady who didn't want to serve with the kids in a hands-on way, but she loved to do administrative tasks. I was able to use her help to create new processes for follow-up. She sent text messages using an app to all the parents of first-time guests, and I received the replies and continued the conversation with the parents. She used the same process for contacting kids who had been missing church for more than 2 weeks. I found out about surgeries and sicknesses that I would have never known about without that process in place. That is just one example of a process that was developed with a growth mindset. There are a host of other processes that helped us grow from one size to the next. The key is to always keep a growth mindset.

It doesn't matter if you are serving in a church that has 15 attendees or 15,000, churches of all sizes need to be served well by their pastors and leaders. Use these five ways I've shared in this chapter to minister to your people well. Remember to always align with the vision of your pastor, evaluate where you are and where you want to go, identify your priorities and make a plan, build relationships with people, and put processes in place that will help you accomplish all that God has set before you.

Do it all with this familiar verse as your main focus. "Seek first His kingdom and His righteousness, and all these things will be added to you." Matthew 6:33 (NIV)

3 Questions to Ask Yourself

1. What is your lead pastor's vision for the ministry of the church, and how does it align with the vision God has placed on your heart?

2. What are the top three areas within your ministry that need urgent attention?

3. Who are some key or potential volunteers who you could build a relationship with?

First Step

Write down the first step you need to take to set up your ministry for success.

_____

_____

About Jeffrey

Jeffrey Hunter is an experienced kids' and lead pastor. By a divine calling, Jeff is coaching the next generation of leaders, following mentorship under Jim Wideman. He's a seasoned speaker at kids' camps, conventions, conferences, and evangelistic services, known for his innovative use of visual and creative methods in Gospel presentations. With three decades of expertise in clowning, puppetry, illusion, storytelling, and multimedia, booking Jeff guarantees a dynamic addition to your event. Learn more about Jeffrey at:

TheMarkMinistries.com

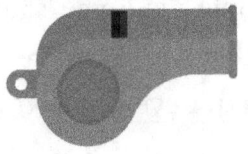

14
Leading as a Young Leader
Emily Saum

Do you have a nickname? Here's another question for you: Do you have a nickname only one person uses for you? I've had many different ones. Here are some of mine. Em and Emi are a couple of common ones, but then it gets a little unique from there. My grandpa has always called me Sweetie Pie. When I lived in Uganda, my Ugandan name was Nalalungi. And somehow, my aunt always called me Hamster… not sure where that came from. But my favorite of all would be what my dad called me: Daughter. All my life until he went to heaven, he called me Daughter. It was actually uncommon for him to call me Emily. It's always been Daughter to the point that people we knew started calling me Daughter. To this day, there are still a couple of people who aren't even related to me who call me Daughter.

Here are truths I've learned that strengthen me to lead well as a young ministry leader.

1. Who called you?

It didn't matter where I was, if I heard "Hey, Daughter," I didn't even have to turn around to see who was calling me. I immediately knew that my dad was calling me. I knew his voice. It's the same with our Heavenly Father. He's calling out to us. It doesn't matter if you are 15 or 55, you can listen to the Holy Spirit speaking to you. He will give direction. Aren't you thankful that the Holy Spirit doesn't wait until you are at a certain age to speak to you? The question is: Are you listening? We see in 1 Samuel chapter 3 that as a young boy, God spoke to Samuel. That shows me there is no age limit on the people to whom God speaks.

2. Whose are you?

The nickname wasn't just a little silly nickname from my dad. It was also about establishing identity. Every time I heard "Hey, Daughter," I knew whose I was. I was no one else's but his. What an amazing gift that if you are reconciled to God in Christ, you get to be a son or daughter of the Most High. If you are a son or daughter of God, you can carry on in whatever season you are in. Whether you are younger or older, when it comes down to it, you're still a son or daughter. What a privilege and honor you get to have! He gave the right for you to be a child of God. "But to all who believed him and accepted him, he gave the right to become children of God" John 1:12 (NIV).

3. Walk in obedience

Now, being a child of God also means coming under authority. When you come under authority, it brings protection and blessings that you would not have otherwise. Of course, there were times when my dad needed to have a talking with me. Did I like it at the time? Of course not. Do I appreciate it now? 100%. Why did he do that? Because he cared for my best interest. There are going to be times when you don't understand things. Walk in obedience. Do it anyway. Especially for a young leader in ministry, it can be easy to think you've got it all figured out, and when someone comes alongside and has a "come-to-Jesus" meeting with you, it's easy to react in ways that aren't healthy for your growth. I encourage you to walk in humble obedience. On the flip side, as you get older, you can tend to think you've seen it all. I've got news for you, you haven't. Let Him exceed your expectations. You will be blessed because of it.

Jesus teaches in John 14:15 that if you love Him, you will keep His commandments. That applies to all of us. None of us are exempt.

4. Walk outside the comfort zone

We all have things we like and things we want to do. It's easy to get comfortable. I have always had this tug-of-war with anything outside my comfort zone. I hate it and love it all at the same time. At 12 years old, I got on a plane to Uganda with my grandpa, leaving my parents and siblings for a month, terrified. But I knew it was right. That initial trip drastically changed my life. It led to me eventually living there and really taught me how to live outside of my comfort zone as a way of life. I look back and see how God uses people in my life to push me to go where the Lord was calling me. Whether it was, "Hey, Daughter, you're going to lead the chapel services this week at camp" or "You got this, I'm here for you" encouragements from many friends and mentors. But so far, I haven't seen God's faithfulness change just because I get a little nervous or haven't reached a certain age. God has been faithful to walk with me outside that comfort zone. Over and over again, I've chosen to walk into the uncomfortable and not wait until I got a little older. I think of Esther, this young girl who chose to step out and save her people. God placed her in that position, but she still had to take the step.

5. Walk in confidence

Growing up, I was a pretty shy and nervous girl. Traveling with my family as children's evangelists and flying to Uganda all the time put this shy girl in scary places at times. It would've been very easy for me to say, "Someone else can do that." No, no, no, God called me. I am His. That changes everything. I remember when the Holy Spirit filled me up with His presence. There was a boldness I couldn't shake. This shy girl suddenly was going after it. That's walking in confidence. I remember at 24, when my dad passed away, having to make a decision: Do I continue in ministry even though my dad is gone? Through my tears, I stood on that stage for my dad's memorial and said, "I'll do it; it's my turn. Ministry isn't going to stop." That's walking in confidence. That's knowing you are a daughter of the King. Things happen, you get older, change comes, but none of that really stands a chance when you have the confidence from the Lord.

There are two people in the Bible who you don't hear many sermons about. But these two are some of my favorites: Simeon and Anna. In Luke 2, they stayed faithful to the end, and they were able to see the Messiah with their own eyes. Do you want to be like that? Keep walking in that confidence from the Lord. Nowhere in God's Word do I see anything about an age limit. You don't have to wait to reach an age to lead, and you can't age out either. Actually, Joel 2:28 says that the old men will dream dreams and the young men will see visions. There it is.

3 Questions to Ask Yourself

1. What is stopping you from walking boldly into where God is taking you?

2. In this season, who can you learn from who is older and younger than you?

3. How can you thrive at your current age?

First Step

What is the first step you need to take to lead well in your current season?

_____

_____

About Emily

Emily Saum has dedicated her life to ministry, continuing a legacy inherited from her family. Her grandfather was a pioneer children's evangelist, and Emily spent her childhood traveling the world with her family, who also focused on children's evangelism, ministering in churches and camps. Her passion for helping children led her to Uganda, where she served as the resident director of a babies' home. Today, Emily serves as the Middle School Pastor at Mount Paran Church in Atlanta, Georgia. Contact Emily at:

emilysaum@me.com

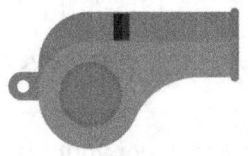

15
Making Your Service Dazzle
Tyler Thompson

I love a good experience, whether it's a movie, a trip, or a theme park. I am intrigued by all of the things that make it happen. What registers as a good experience to me is when your expectations are exceeded, you leave wanting more (or don't want to leave), and you find yourself telling others about it. When it comes to your service, wouldn't it be great for kids and parents to be blown away by what you offer, becoming raving fans who tell all of their family and friends about how you do ministry? I think it's safe to say that anyone who is in Next Gen ministry of any type wants their service to be the best part of every toddler's, kid's, preteen's, and volunteer's week. I fully believe it's possible.

1. Empower your team

Two things we weren't meant to do alone are life and ministry. No matter how big or small your service is, you are not meant to be the only one doing it. Here's proof: check out Ephesians 4 (NIV). Ministry has been given to each of us. And this interpretation is confirmed when you read verses 11 and 12 in the passage. "And he gave the apostles, the prophets, the evangelists, the shepherds, and teachers, to equip the saints for the work of ministry, for building up the body of Christ." Everyone can play a part. Sure, there are background checks and training, but you'll find that leaning on the gifts and strengths of others will make your experience that much better.

There was a season when it seemed challenging to find people to host from the stage. While talking to some volunteers, we discovered that one of them, who seemed like an introvert, was actually into acting. So, we gave him a script, and during a rehearsal, he took the stage and was a completely different person. I found that most people just need to be given a chance. I know what you're thinking; I promise you I've been there too, but I wanted to share a quote that changed my perspective: "There was a time when you couldn't do ministry as well as you do now" - Jim Wideman. It couldn't be more true. You weren't born an excellent communicator, worship leader, small group coordinator, etc. Someone gave you a chance and empowered you to take your place in ministry. Who do you need to give opportunities to? Following this step isn't just a good idea. You will see God bring more people your way when you steward the ones that you serve. Luke 16:10 (NASB) says, "The one who is faithful in a very little thing is also faithful in much; and the one who is unrighteous in a very little thing is also unrighteous in much."

2. Have you created a space where they can encounter God?

This one is the key. If this doesn't happen, you don't have a service. It doesn't matter how great your room looks, how technologically advanced your equipment is, or how even Disney is jealous of your stage experience. If you haven't provided a space where kids encounter God, all you did was entertain. Themes, decor, songs, and groups are all great elements to point kids to Jesus. The world can compete with those four things, and toe to toe, we would lose. But the "trump card" or the "Draw 4" over any "experience" is an "encounter" with Jesus. These people had encounters: Jairus, the woman with the issue of blood (Luke 8:41-46), the woman at the well, the rest of the town (John 4:1-42), and even the disciples.

1 John 1:1-6 (NIV) says, "That which was from the beginning, which we have heard, which we have seen with our eyes, which we looked upon and have touched with our hands,

concerning the word of life, the life was made manifest, and we have seen it, and testify to it and proclaim to you the eternal life, which was with the Father and was made manifest to us that which we have seen and heard we proclaim also to you, so that you too may have fellowship with us, and indeed our fellowship is with the Father and with His Son Jesus Christ." It was the encounter that they had with Jesus that led them to live out what God had called them to do. You have the opportunity; you have been entrusted with that for the kids you serve. Themes and decor should provide a bridge to help kids understand the Bible. Songs should lead kids from excitement to being engaged in knowing how to worship and experience the presence of God. The message and the small groups should be places where kids see real-life examples of what it looks like to have a relationship with Jesus. Long after they've gone through the ministry, kids and students will forget the glow sticks hanging from the ceiling, the motions to the songs, but they won't forget the time they first felt the presence of God during worship or when they saw a prayer answered in a small group.

3. Begin with the end in mind: What results are we expecting?

Orlando is the ideal destination for many. Before I step in my car, I've already pulled out my phone and put my destination in Google Maps. Knowing these two things will take your service to the next level: knowing the destination and the directions to get there. Knowing the destination is the best place to start. Start with the end in mind. Often times throughout scripture, when God called someone to do something, He gave them a vision of the end result. For Moses, it was freedom for the Israelites and the Promised Land. For Joseph, it was his leadership impacting his family. Planning has to go before action. Envision what you want the service to look like. What do you want the kids to leave not just knowing but applying? How do you want to start the service? What activity helps the kids feel welcome? What songs need to be part of your service? What examples and illustrations do you need to include? How can you incorporate tech and media to connect with the kids and students on their level?

4. That was great! What did you do?

"That was the best service yet!" "Service was so awesome!" "My child won't stop talking about kids' church!" This is what you may hear from volunteers, families, and fellow staff. My response to that is always two things: Gratitude for what took place and also thankfulness for what they shared. Secondly, I ask "Why?"

Why was it the best service ever? What made this particular service shine? What is it about the service that the child won't stop talking about? Success leaves clues. One of my favorite John Maxwell quotes is, "Experience isn't the best teacher, evaluated experience is."

What made it great? Did you switch something in the service flow? Did you add a devotional to the pre-service huddle? Was it the extra time you took to pray over the families and volunteers? Was it the life change story you shared in the team group text that fired up the team? Was it sending a video to the team instead of just a wordy email? Who did you call and check on that was the tipping point for the team?

Whenever my parents said my name twice, I knew they meant business. It's even more so when God says something twice. Haggai 1:5-7 (NIV) says, "Now therefore, thus says the Lord of hosts, 'Consider your ways! You have sown much, but harvest little; you eat, but there is not enough to be satisfied; you drink, but there is not enough to become drunk; you put on clothing, but no one is warm enough; and he who earns, earns wages to put into a purse with holes.' Thus says the Lord of hosts, 'Consider your ways!'"

To add it a third time: consider your ways. Why are 5th graders tuning out? Why do the 1st graders think the first song for worship means it's time to play tag?

I'm sure you have a structure to your service; you may be the G.O.A.T. of Planning Center. But evaluated experience can lead to making changes that make your service that much better.

5. What's everyone else doing?

Maybe not everyone, but what are other ministries and companies doing that you can add to your service experience to make it that much better? You don't have to learn from your experience alone; you can learn from the experiences of others. Who are your others? When I attend a conference I enjoy reaching out to the staff outside of the conference to ask them what their service flow looked like and why they did it that way. Facebook, TikTok, and Instagram have made it even easier to explore what others are doing. Most churches have accounts where they're posting certain parts of their service. You can up your research game by creating lists and saving posts and reels you come across.

Then there are others outside of the church. Why do people shop at Target like they do? What are some of your favorite places to spend your time outside of your home? An easy place to quadruple your research is to look at Disney. They pay thousands upon thousands of dollars to a team to research sights, sounds, and smells. It's free game.

3 Questions to Ask Yourself

1. What is a programming element you've experienced at an event that you could adjust to use in your Sunday Morning Large Group time?

2. Do you want your kids to leave your services with a good experience or a God experience? What pieces are missing?

3. What system could you put in place to evaluate your service? What worked, what didn't work, and what never needs to happen again?

First Step

What's your first step in making your service dazzle?

_____

_____

About Tyler

Tyler Thompson has been in Next Gen ministry for more than 20 years. As a seasoned freelance creative, he brings a unique blend of innovation and experience to his work. As a ministry coach, he provides both group and individual sessions to empower and equip leaders. You can connect with Tyler at:

    levelupkidmin@gmail.com

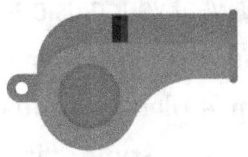

16
Making Worship Better
Yancy Wideman Richmond

I love leading kids in worship. I believe kids are the easiest age group to lead in worship. Why? Because it's naturally in us to worship and kids are the closest to the beginning point of how God designed us all to live. The more conversations I have with leaders like you, the more I realize so many of the issues we face are the same. So much of problem-solving *why* you're not getting the type of engagement you long for during worship is fundamentally because of these five components. Of course, there can be other nuances and tweaks to be made in *how* you lead or *what* you present, but the foundation of it all begins with these five ingredients.

1. Identify what your music sounds like.

Not all music for kids is created equal. Let's be honest, there's plenty of music for kids that sounds kiddie. Sadly, some of it sounds like nails on a chalkboard. Quality sound recordings and styles matter. For this generation to take it seriously, it must resemble the high quality, catchy sound of pop music. It should sound "normal." Kids' music can get a bad rap because it sounds lesser than. I have noticed kids' musical tastes are more mature than most adults think it is. It's definitely more mature than a lot of children's ministry leaders are aware. The elements of the song you need to consider as age-appropriate for your group include:

- **Vocabulary**: They need to understand the words.
- **Singability**: Is it catchy? Are lines or sections of the song repeated? Repetition is so helpful in leading children.
- **Arrangement**: Consider things like the beat, tempo, and vocal range of

the song.
- **Length**: Consider their attention spans. Is the song too long?

Now could be a great time to evaluate the music you've been using in your ministry. You may feel unequipped to do this. That's ok. Get some of your other leaders involved. If you work with preteens, get students involved. Play them recordings. Allow them to help you research and choose new options that may be the perfect fit for your ministry. Make sure whatever you present shows kids that Jesus is relevant to their lives. This is a value I always want to be true in what I present through the songs I lead.

2. Get someone to lead them.

Videos do not lead worship FOR you. They are a wonderful asset and incredible tool that you have in ministry. Think of them as an accessory because that's what they are. A video alone will never lead the worship for you. Don't press play and walk away.

You need a person leading them. Musical talent is a huge win here, but you don't have to limit yourself to that. I have found leading worship is more about your leadership ability than your musical ability. You need someone who can set up and segue between songs, cultivate space for kids to experience God's presence, pray into the song set, and lead the kids in your ministry. Guess what? None of those are musical things. If the person can learn the arrangements of the songs and have something prepared to encourage everyone in an attitude of worship, they are worship leader material. If they can find ways to engage and encourage participation then they can make a great worship leader for kids. Psalm 47:1 (NLT) is a great example of what the role of a worship leader is: "Come, everyone! Clap your hands! Shout to God with joyful praise!"

3. Teach them about worship.

Believe it or not, this is something that so often gets left out. Are you just doing songs in your ministry? Or are you leading kids in worship? Your leader should be giving little nuggets of information and wisdom about worship each week. They should share what worship looks like in the life of a believer. Share how they can get involved. Let them know why their worship matters. So often you lead songs without first teaching why we worship God. Help kids choose to worship the Lord.

A verse we all know that I strongly believe applies to this topic is Hosea 4:6 (NIV), "My people are destroyed from lack of knowledge." Give your kids understanding and revelation about worship and watch connection unfold and flourish.

4. Change things up by introducing something new.

When was the last time you introduced something new? Was it last year at VBS? Have you introduced anything new since camp? Introducing new things is hard. It takes time to research and find the songs. It involves financial investment to purchase new resources. It requires more time to learn the song well and be prepared. Consistently evaluating and editing what songs are working well and what needs to get a rest or even be put on a "don't sing anymore" list needs to be a reoccurring thing on your to-do list. Maybe it's something you evaluate monthly or at least quarterly.

It's the difference between stagnant water and fresh water. Which one would you choose to drink from? Introducing something new is a great way to insert some excitement and energy. I believe it will breathe life into your times of worship. Realize it will require repeating the song the first several weeks in a row and singing it pretty regularly the first couple months for everyone to catch on. Allow for the repetition. Find ways to let the song be heard on playlists pre/post service or that you send home with families via a QR code/link. Singing new songs is a biblical practice. You can't afford to not make space for new.

5. Consider your invitation.

What are you inviting them to take part in? Have you ever considered what you're wanting to ask the kids to do while participating in worship? Say more than "Now it's time to sing!" Some of your students will respond with a "So what?" Even if it's silent, you know they do, based on their actions. Start to define what your vision is for worship and make it specific to each set. What type of posture are you hoping to see? What actions can you encourage? How can you connect some dots for revelation to occur in their minds and spirits? Intentionally invite them into a time of worship every time you gather. Remind them of why it matters. Practically break down what a sacrifice of praise could look like today.

There is **so much more** awaiting you at the table. It's time to pull up a chair and get ready to partake of all God has for you as you lead His creation to give Him praise .

3 Questions to Ask Yourself

1. How does your church place value on worship and use worship to raise up Christ-followers?

2. How are you cultivating a love for the Father through the expression of songs sung, knees bowed down, hands extended with reverence, and time spent in His presence?

3. What is your vision for helping kids hunger and thirst for more of Jesus?

First Step

What's your first step to make worship better?

_____

_____

About Yancy

Yancy Wideman Richmond is a worship leader, songwriter, and author who makes Jesus loud. Her Dove Award winning music helps kids fall in love with Jesus one song at a time. Every week her songs are used in thousands of churches globally. She is a passionate advocate of raising disciples to worship. She authored the book *Sweet Sound: The Power of Discipling Kids in Worship*. Yancy and her family live in Nashville, TN.

Learn more about CHORUS, her Worship Leader Coaching for Next Gen Ministry at:

YancyMinistries.com/coaching

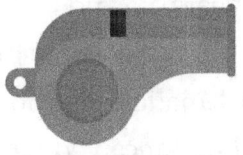

17
Bridging the Gap Between Kids and Students
Corinne Noble

Preteens can be a tough age group to effectively minister to. They are often still included in kids' ministry, although some larger churches have been able to separate them out into their own ministry. We have the challenge of simultaneously trying to make our kids' ministry relevant for them while creating a sturdy bridge for them to transition smoothly into the youth/student ministry. This age group may not be the easiest to reach, but they are worth the extra effort to find ways to help them bridge the gap. I've always had a huge place in my heart for this age group. I received my call to be a kids' pastor when I was 10 years old and in the 5th grade. My whole life course was altered in that moment and every decision I made going forward revolved around the calling I received when I was in this pivotal age group.

Let's talk about five proven ways to help bridge the gap between kids' and student ministries and stop preteens from falling through the cracks.

1. Provide ministry that is aimed at preteens

I've heard a lot of ministries giving up on this age group, just assuming the student ministry can deal with them in the next year or two. I believe we are losing a lot of kids in this age range because we aren't going to the extra effort to engage them on their level. We need to stop saying things like, "They have just outgrown kids' ministry" and "They have just checked out." It's our responsibility to offer ministry that is aimed at preteen's interests and age level. It doesn't require a separate environment, more volunteers, or a bigger budget to begin doing this. Those things are nice, but if you don't have them, here are some ways to start engaging preteens without them. Always aim at the oldest kids in the room and make your ministry boy-friendly. Look at every element in your ministry and ask yourself this question: "Would the oldest boy in my ministry like this?" If the answer is no, then scrap it or adapt it.

2. Create opportunities for relationships to form

Utilize small groups to create a place for kids to form relationships. If you have the space/resources, make a preteen small group environment that they would want to be in. Think games, video games, couches/bean bag chairs, and no "cheesy" décor. Don't depend on your weekend services to reach this age group effectively. Remember, relationship and belonging are the most important things to this age group. If preteens don't have friends and feel like they belong at church, they won't care what you are teaching or doing. They won't want to be there. That's why it's so important to create opportunities for preteens to connect outside of normal service times. Most churches have small groups that meet offsite throughout the week for adults, so why shouldn't you offer them for kids and student ministries as well? One of the most effective ways I have kept preteens engaged and loving being in church was through offering an offsite small group just for them once a month in my home. The kids who came to this group found friends and loved coming to church. I have done scavenger hunts themed around upcoming holidays, movie nights, game nights, and pool parties. Just keep it basic and leave lots of space for talking and forming friendships.

3. Give them a place to serve

I know many churches want kids to wait until they are in middle school or even high school to start serving, but I believe that kids have so much to offer right now. Many of them are beginning to discover their strengths and talents already outside of the church through sports and activities, so why not in the church? They are more willing to serve now than they would be in a couple of years. Create a culture of serving in the hearts of your kids and after a few years you will have built your own ministry team. Almost all of the kids who have started serving as kids have come back to serve as teenagers in my ministries. Most importantly, the kids who served are the ones still going to church and pursuing a relationship with Jesus. Empower your kids to be a part of serving the church right now and they will have a heart for serving for life.

4. Don't isolate your ministry from the rest of the church

It is easy to become isolated on your own ministry islands (kids, preteens, and student ministries), but it is not beneficial to your ministries or the kids you are leading. Pay attention to what the other ministries in the church are doing and offer similar ministry options and events. Use some of the same worship songs and do teaching series together. When your kids and student ministries look so drastically different from each other, it's not surprising that kids would have a hard time making the transition from one ministry to the next. Find ways to unify kids' and student ministries and make it easy for kids to move up.

5. Find ways to partner with each other

Kids' and student ministries should not be in competition or working against one another. The kids' and student ministries should be partners, cheering each other on, helping each other out, and working together to create the bridge, if possible. If this is not the case at your church, that's the best place to start building the bridge or repairing it, if necessary. If you are the kids' pastor/director, invite the student ministries pastor to speak in your kids' or preteen services on a regular basis. The kids' and student ministry leaders should meet regularly to find out what they are doing and see how you can work together to make each other's ministries successful.

Our main goal should always be to keep preteens engaged and loving coming to church, and to provide a smooth and healthy transition for them into the student ministry.

It can be done! After years of implementing these principles, I have seen preteen ministries flourish, kids love being in kids' ministry to the very last day, and kids moving up to the student ministries with friends while plugging in right away. I've seen them grow and continue to serve in the church well after they leave kids' and student ministries. This age group is worth the extra effort, so let's stop allowing them to slip through the cracks.

3 Questions to Ask Yourself

1. What are some of the "cracks in the bridge" between kids' and student ministries in your church?

2. How can you create more opportunities for kids and students to form meaningful relationships?

3. What are some ways you can start partnering with other ministries in the church to create a "sturdier bridge"?

First Step

What's the first step you are going to take to build a better bridge between the ministries in your church to keep kids from falling through the cracks?

_____

_____

About Corinne

Corinne Noble is the founder of Kidmin Corinne Ministries. Corinne and her husband, Sean, love traveling and doing ministry as a team. She enjoys speaking, coaching, and creating resources for kidmin leaders at:

kidmincorinne.com

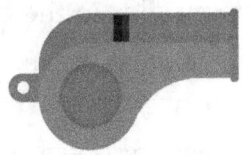

18
Say "No" to Silos
Stacey Brooks

Attending a concert at the local art center to hear an orchestra play is one of my favorite things to do. I love it as they warm up. You can hear each instrument individually tuning and preparing for the beautiful music to come. Each instrument is needed to make the orchestra complete. Each score is composed of many complex parts that blend together to deliver a rich experience for all who are listening. Each musician plays at their top capacity so everyone shines. In the same way, the church should be in harmony, not just "perform" many solos within different departments at the same time. These solos are often referred to as silos in the church, and we must learn to break them down.

1. Everything starts with a leader.

In an orchestra it starts with the conductor, or in our world, the lead pastor. Staff meetings or ministry reports can set the tone for how ministry is conducted. Instead of allowing statements like "my budget" or "my volunteers", the staff should be trained to change the language and mentality of how they see resources, spaces, and even people. Celebrating how you see God at work using the resources He has given to bless the church will start to strengthen the church family. You will see how God is using each instrument to accomplish His purpose.

2. Look at your spaces

As you look around, do your spaces create natural silos? Are all of your offices by department only, or are there collaborative spaces? Do the flyers on the Connect Counter all start with the ministry first or the church name and then the ministry conducting the event? Does each ministry have a separate logo or are they all tied into the church branding? Are the rooms in the building labeled by who uses the space or are they identified in a way that feels welcoming to everyone? This is a difficult survey to take, but very necessary. How you answer these questions will set the tone for only "solos" within the church or for a full rich "performance" by all.

3. Less is more

Take a good hard look at the events that have made it to your church calendar. Ask yourself if the events pull the church family apart or do they allow for multigenerational relationships to be formed and fostered. The answer to this question should not add more events for your congregation, but see where you can tweak it for training, equipping, and involving everyone. Here's an example. Your church has an Awana Ministry for kids the same night that adult Bible

Studies are going on. Invite your adults to be the verse listeners for the kids and have the kids be the verse listeners for the adults. Everyone is in the building at the same time, but this will break down silos of adult versus children's ministry. It is now discipleship classes in multiple rooms for multiple people of all ages on the same night. Little tweaks like that can have a deep impact on how you do ministry and how it is received and perceived by all involved.

4. Clear communication is key

You have all played the game of Telephone sometime in your life. It is so funny when the message gets to the very end, and it's all tangled up, not even close to what the message started out to be. The game is fun, but in ministry, where the communication needs to be clear and accurate, it is not so comical. In fact, it can be detrimental. When ministries are operating in the silo mentality, it can be very difficult to get the details accurately and timely to all the places and people who need to know. This can cause major frustration among the staff, which can lead to further division instead of the desired outcome of harmony and teamwork. When ministry is planned as a whole, everyone can be part of the process which can lead to clarity in communication.

5. Seamless movements

As you are listening to a beautifully composed piece of music, you can detect where one instrument passes the lead to another. It makes each movement stronger and the music richer. In ministry, you need to learn to pass the melody from section to section in the same way. There are natural progressions within the church where there is movement between ministries. As life stages happen, so do transitions. Children will move to student ministry and student ministry to adult ministry. As a church, you need to make this movement as seamless as possible.

In a church where silos have been removed, the planning for this movement has been thoroughly anticipated. When the "my" ministry has been replaced with "our" ministry, it becomes seamless. As a church, you need to create a cohesive plan from birth to 18, including milestones that are celebrated by the church as a whole. This gives room and opportunity for the body of Christ to serve together. When the student pastor and volunteer team have already created relationships with the children moving into middle school, it is a natural progression instead of one filled with anxiety of the unknown for both the students and parents. The same principle applies to all areas of transition. When you learn to serve with one another and for one another, the church is in full and beautiful harmony

Specialized ministries and departments can be beneficial within an organization or church. You can be focused and deliberate with the resources used, as well as the teams that are developed. However, when the "us" versus "them" mentality seeps in, it can cause division, competitiveness, and pride that can divide and ultimately destroy the ministry. The most beautiful part of the concert is when all sections are balanced in order to complement the composition as a whole. In the church, when silos are broken down, ministry is more cohesive and the body is more effective for the kingdom.

3 Questions to Ask Yourself

1. How can transitioning from a silo mentality in your church change the effectiveness of the ministry God has entrusted to you?

2. Who do you need to have conversations with about creating seamless movements within your church?

3. What are ways you can tweak your church calendar to include multiple ministries and become a multigenerational church body that is serving together?

First Step

What is your first step to say "no" to the silos in your church?

_____

_____

About Stacey

Stacey Brooks has been in children's ministry for the past three decades. She has served in the local church as both volunteer and paid staff and has been involved with Child Evangelism Fellowship as a local director. Stacey currently lives in the Chicagoland area and is on staff at Harvest Bible Chapel.

She offers individual coaching throughout the year and can be contacted at:

stacey.cm.coach@gmail.com

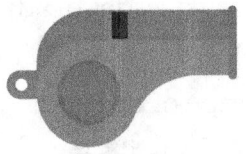

19
Hey Staff, Can We All Get Along?
Jim Wideman

Alright, folks, let's talk about Millennials, the Gens', and the Boomers working together in perfect harmony. What if we build a bridge from the same old ways we've always done church to leading change in order to minister effectively to younger families? Yes, I hear some of you younger leaders out there groaning, "That just sounds painful." "Boomers are set in their ways and they don't want to hear what younger leaders have to say." That might be true in some churches, but it doesn't have to be true everywhere. At my church we have intentionally built a close culture where each generation is valued and is working hard at working together.

Through my decades of adventures in ministry—from bell-bottoms to TikTok dances—I've seen the landscape of church and family change dramatically. And yes, it's important you change with the times to reach today's young families and disciple today's kids. But while you adapt your methods, you must hold on to the timeless, never-changing, ever-current good news of the gospel of Jesus Christ. That is the legacy each of us should be working toward.

So, before we dive into the deep end, let's get our definitions straight. Mr. Webster defines legacy as "the long-lasting impact of particular events, actions, etc. that took place in the past, or in a person's life." Every event, every program, every service you have has one purpose: to make disciples of kids and leaders for life. To pull this off, you have to be intentional about building generational bridges and working together. I'm talking about working together through your age, cultural, and generational differences to build a dynamic multi-generational staff and volunteer team.

Churches and families looked a whole lot different when I started working in churches. Churches today are more diverse than ever. But there's a new kind of diversity that you must address head-on to leave a lasting legacy: generational diversity. Baby Boomers, Gen-Xers, Millennials, and Gen-Zers now coexist in your church staffs, each bringing their own unique perspectives, work styles, and values. Here are five things you can do now to bridge these generational gaps and work better together.

1. Understand the generational mixtape

Each generation's got its own vibe. Baby Boomers are the loyal workhorses. Gen Xers are the cool, balanced types, always seeking a life outside the office. Millennials? They're all about teamwork and finding purpose. And Gen Z, bless their hearts, they can't imagine a world without wi-fi. But here's the kicker: we're better together! No one generation has all the answers. It's important to acknowledge and appreciate these differences because each generation brings something valuable to the table. You can make a greater impact for the kingdom when you put your heads together rather than working apart.

2. Let's all get along, shall we?

Creating a church staff and volunteer teams where every age feels like they've got a seat at the table is key. In my weekly one-on-ones with younger staff, they've taught me so much! I've learned about apps I need to incorporate on all my devices and how to embrace AI as a tool to work smarter. We all can help each other. By promoting cross-generational dialogue and learning, you can harness the collective wisdom of multiple generations to drive innovation and growth within your teams. Every age group must value the other and realize God has brought you all together to learn from one another for a reason. Be open to learning from each team member regardless of age and never think your way is the only way.

3. Curiosity didn't kill the cat; it made things interesting

There's always something new to pick up, no matter your age. I learn something every day if I want to, and believe me, I want to! Let's approach interactions with all generations with a sense of curiosity and open-mindedness, embracing the opportunities to gain new insights and perspectives from one another. What can you do to embrace curiosity and open-mindedness on your team? I've found it starts with spending time with them. At Conduit Church I am the oldest on staff. Each Tuesday we go to lunch as a staff. It's not mandatory but it's encouraged. The youngest folks on staff never miss and they come up with the place. I go and I learn through their lens of life and work. I've found being open to learning from other generations is the first step to seeing it take place.

4. Be all ears

Everyone wants to feel heard. So, let's actually listen. Ask the younger crowd for their take and maybe, just maybe, pick their brains on a solution that needs to be implemented. Just as Boomers have stories to share, so do younger generations. Let's listen to their perspectives with empathy and understanding, creating a space where they feel heard and valued. Younger leaders thrive on being asked for their input. Choose their ideas whenever possible to show them their input is valuable. Go back and read these last two sentences about 10 more times until they sink in. In fact, if you are a book highlighter like me, those two sentences are gold.

5. Embrace change

The world is spinning fast, and we've got to keep up. Being open to new ideas and tech doesn't mean you're selling out; it means you're tuning in. Each generation must embrace change with open arms. By staying open to new ideas and technologies, you can remain relevant and model openness and adaptability. The more you model being open to change, the more those around you will show openness to change.

There you have it—five no-sweat strategies for building generational bridges. Building generational bridges within your church teams isn't just about making everyone feel included; it's about creating value and respect within each generation, seeking to understand the differences, and celebrating what you have in common. You can leave a lasting legacy that transcends age barriers. By applying these strategies, you can ensure that everyone on your teams feels valued, heard, and empowered to work together to contribute to the legacy you all leave behind through your united efforts to build the kingdom of God. Let's blend our tunes, learn from each other, and leave a mark that'll have future generations talking (and maybe even dancing). Let's get to it!

3 Questions to Ask Yourself

1. Are all generations in your church represented with a seat around your leadership table?

2. Do you ask questions to younger staff and team in order to learn from them on a regular basis? If not, how can you start this week?

3. What is the greatest piece of advise or wisdom you've learned from a Boomer? Have you ever told them thanks? Will you?

First Step

Now, my favorite part—identifying your first step. What will be your first step to work together better with your staff and team?

_____

_____

About Jim

Jim Wideman has been helping ministry leaders thrive for a half century. He's currently The Executive Pastor of Ministries at Conduit Church in Franklin, Tennessee. He also offers group and individual coaching throughout the year and has authored over 15 books for NextGen ministry. Find out more about his resources and coaching at:

jimwideman.com

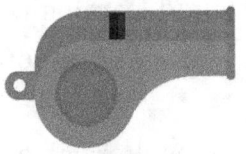

20
Applying What You've Learned
Jim Wideman

I am a lifetime learner. I have not arrived! God is not finished with us yet. We are all a work in progress. But I learned years ago some learners make more progress, faster than others! That's because they want to. I have found in my years of coaching, some people want to learn more than others. If you've ever heard me teach before or read any of my other books, you have heard me say, "You can learn something everyday if you want to, and believe me I WANT TO!"

I have found out it's up to me to be on the lookout of what and who I can learn from. I've learned from every person and every group I've coached. It is the responsibility of a leader to be a learner. I have found learning without applying what I am learning slows me down from achieving my goals.

I am a very goal-oriented person. One of my favorite quotes from my book *Tweetable Leadership* is, "If you aim at nothing, you'll hit it every time." I used to be one of those people who had a goal for everything. I loved checking things off my to-do list. I still do. But then I started learning about the power of evaluation which led to asking myself three questions.

1. What do I need to be learning?
2. What is the priority of this goal or task? When I started setting goals and making improvements by priority, I began to see and notice the difference. So did others.
3. What are the best ways to apply what I'm learning?

Learning something new is exciting, not scary. Here's a great place for an attitude adjustment. Give yourself a check-up from the neck up and see where you need to correct your thinking. I have found the real magic happens when you start applying the new thing you're learning in fun and creative ways. Here are five strategies I used to bring my newfound knowledge to life and keep the learning process moving in the right direction.

1. Become the teacher

Channel your inner professor and share your new skills with others. It's not just about reinforcing your knowledge; studying something to teach and making the presentation is one of the best ways to make the new information my own. When I first started learning about leadership, this was a real game changer for me. I started teaching what I was learning to my staff and key volunteers. I created a once-a-month Sunday night get-together I called The Children's Ministry Leadership Club. It started with a few and then morphed into a hundred. I later started making those lessons available by subscription where I was reaching thousands of kidmin leaders long before podcasts were a thing. Those lessons turned into books and I'm still doing that today, taking what I'm learning and teaching it to others.

2. Incorporate learning into your daily routine

Make your daily grind a lot more exciting by sneaking in your new skills in creative ways. For me, it all starts with my calendar. Every day I end my day with evaluation and looking ahead at tomorrow. Where can I add what I'm learning into tomorrow's agenda? Where can I set aside time to practice this new skill or study it more fully. I use an app called Todoist. I like it because it sounds like King James (LOL). I can have separate to-do lists for each of my projects, but it also can be sorted by day. I incorporate what I'm learning to my to-do lists as well. Remember what a wise old man once said, "Same action brings same results!" If you want to see different results, you have to add in new actions!

3. Collaborate and play

Learning doesn't have to be a solo journey. Team up with friends or colleagues and turn collaboration into a fun game. Here's why I like it: Learning becomes a party with friends. Also, collaborating brings fresh, fun perspectives. I am thankful that in my early days of being a children's pastor I had some creative children's pastor friends to brainstorm with. Iron sharpening iron friends who made me better and who told me when my idea needed some work. I always enjoy a little friendly competition to spice things up. By making a game out of it, it's always more fun. Yes, there might be a winner but no one really loses when you make a game out of it.

4. Make yourself accountable by evaluating and asking yourself questions.

I have cut down on the number of books I read each year. Jim, that's not a very good thing to say for a guy who writes books. I've found it's not the amount of books that I read that causes me to grow as a leader. More importantly, it's about applying what I'm learning and using that information to be more effective, not to just check off books from a list. Before you put this book back on the shelf or you go write your Google or Amazon review, go back though the book and look at what you underlined. (I hope you've been underlining as you read.) What is your plan to apply what you underlined? Why did you mark it? What stood out to you? Which of the three questions did you take time to answer? Put a star by the ones you need to apply. How about your first step? Did you do it? Look at the chapters where you know you need to improve and think about what steps 2-5 would be. Make time in your calendar to revisit and add steps 6-10 to incorporate this new information into your life.

5. Don't get weary in well doing.

Look up Galatians 6:9-10 in several different versions. Find the one that speaks this truth the best to you. I love keeping in touch with the people I coach. I am their friend for life, long after they quit paying me. Almost all of them say after a while they just stopped evaluating their time or putting everything in their calendar. They stopped doing what they were doing while I was coaching them and things started getting messy again. Many have signed up to do coaching again or re-read my *Beat The Clock* book. The truth is, they got tired and stopped doing something that was working. Listen friend, it's not the end of the world. Believe me, we've all been there. Just start doing what you know to do again.

For some of you this book was a reminder of things you already knew, but it was a great reminder of what to start doing again. For others you have some new things to try.

Learning is a lifelong adventure, and the best way to enjoy it is by making it fun and engaging. By teaching others, integrating learning into your daily life, collaborating with friends, evaluating and asking questions, and not giving up on things that are working, you can turn the application of knowledge into an exciting journey. But, whatever you do, please don't go alone. Everyone, and I do mean everyone, does better with a coach. If any of us can help you in any way, please reach out!

Meet Jim

Jim Wideman is one of the most recognized and celebrated names in church leadership for a reason. For over half a century he has been a pioneer and leading voice as a pastor, speaker, author, and ministry coach around the world. He continues to blaze new trails by empowering leaders with timeless wisdom, humility, a sharp wit, and refreshing authenticity. He's worked at some of the largest and fastest growing churches in the US, including 17 years leading one of the largest children's ministries in the country. He has published over 15 books, many of which are considered a must have for any Kids Ministry or Family Ministry leader.

Throughout his years of ministry investing in countless children, families, and leaders around the globe; Jim's influence and intentionality has been continuously acknowledged. The

International Network of Children's Ministers (INCM) have awarded Jim both their Ministry of Excellence Award and recently presented Jim with their first-ever Legacy Award for his lifetime achievement in children's ministry. Children's Ministry Magazine has named him as one of the Top 10 Pioneers of the Decade and one of the Top 20 Influencers in Children's Ministry.

Although Jim is thankful for the fruit of past seasons, his commitment to producing fruit in this season is evident in the way he continues to empower others to lead well and helping parents and grandparents thrive in their roles as disciples. His passion to connect the family with Jesus is unparalleled. His family is a beautiful picture of what generational discipleship can look like. He and his lovely bride Julie have been married for over 46 years, have two wonderful daughters and have three of the cutest grandsons ever!

Jim currently serves as the Executive Pastor of Ministries at Conduit Church in Franklin, TN.

Also available from Jim Wideman

Authentic Leadership That Lasts
The "you can do it" guide

Beat The Clock
Successful Strategies for Time Management

Volunteers That Stick

Connect With Your Kids
(Parenting)

Kidmin Leadership

STRETCH
Structuring Your Ministry for Growth

The Eric Trap
5 Things Every Leader Has To Get Right

Tweetable Leadership

For more information about any of these resources, Coaching with Jim, or booking Jim to speak, check out:
jimwideman.com

www.ingramcontent.com/pod-product-compliance
Lightning Source LLC
Chambersburg PA
CBHW071909290426
44110CB00013B/1332